40 HADITH FROM

Sunan al Nasa'i

SHAHRUL HUSSAIN
& ZAHED FETTAH

Forty Hadith from Sunan al-Nasā'ī

First Published in 2023 by
THE ISLAMIC FOUNDATION

Distributed by
KUBE PUBLISHING LTD
Tel +44 (0)1530 249230
E-mail: info@kubepublishing.com
Website: www.kubepublishing.com

Author Shahrul Hussain & Zahed Fettah
Editor Umm Marwan Ibrahim
Cover Design Afreen Fazil (Jaryah Studios)
Arabic/English layout & design Nasir Cadir

A Cataloguing-in-Publication Data record for this book is available from the British Library

ISBN 978-0-86037-975-1
eISBN 978-0-86037-980-5

Printed by Elma Basim, Turkey

Dedication

For Dr Wahabalbari Ahmed
for everything you have done for me

Contents

	Introduction	vii
	Acknowledgments	x
	A Brief Biography of Imam al-Nasā'ī	xi
Hadith 1:	Asking for Power and Authority	1
Hadith 2:	The Virtues of Converting to Islam	4
Hadith 3:	The Things to Seek Refuge in Allah From	7
Hadith 4:	Washing Hands before Dipping them into the Water Vessel	11
Hadith 5:	Virtues of Voluntary Worship (*Nawāfil*)	13
Hadith 6:	Just About Catching the Prayer	16
Hadith 7:	The Forbidden Times to Pray	18
Hadith 8:	Building Grand Mosques: A Sign of the Day of Judgement	21
Hadith 9:	The Construction History of the Three Sacred Mosques	24
Hadith 10:	Superstition in Islam	27
Hadith 11:	Wishing for Death	30
Hadith 12:	Funeral Prayer in Absentia	33
Hadith 13:	When Does the Month of Ramadan Start?	36
Hadith 14:	Fasting One Day for the Sake of Allah	39
Hadith 15:	The Best Fast	41
Hadith 16:	Six Most Wretched People	44
Hadith 17:	The Virtues of *al-Hajj al-Mabrūr*	48
Hadith 18:	False Piety	51
Hadith 19:	Wedding Celebrations	54

Hadith 20: Forced Marriage in Islam 56
Hadith 21: The Mourning Period 59
Hadith 22: Obedience to the Leader is a Must 62
Hadith 23: Bad Rulers 64
Hadith 24: Target Practice and Looking after Living Creatures 67
Hadith 25: Splitting of the Chest 69
Hadith 26: Work and Earnings 71
Hadith 27: Abundance of Wealth and Trading: Signs of the Day of Judgement 73
Hadith 28: Dyeing the Hair 76
Hadith 29: There is no Harm in a Woman Asking a Man to Marry Her 79
Hadith 30: The Seven People who will be Under the Shade of Allah's Throne 82
Hadith 31: How to Solve Problems 85
Hadith 32: What to Recite for Protection and Help 88
Hadith 33: Seeking Refuge in Allah from Hardship and Doing Wrong 91
Hadith 34: The Three *Du'ā's* of Prophet Sulayman 93
Hadith 35: Forgetting to Pray 96
Hadith 36: Greeting Friends in Prayer 98
Hadith 37: Islam: The Complete Religion 100
Hadith 38: Abu Bakr and the Prophet ﷺ as Imam 103
Hadith 39: The Best Fast and the Best Prayer 107
Hadith 40: Treating All Your Children Equally 109

Introduction

All praise is due to Allah, the Lord of the universe, the Most Merciful the Most Kind, the Master of the Day of Judgement. Peace and blessings be upon Muhammad ﷺ, the final Prophet of Allah, and upon his family and Companions.

Hadith is one of the most important institutions in Islam. It contains the teachings of the Prophet Muhammad ﷺ regarding all aspects of Islam. It is indispensable in order to attain the correct understanding of the religion, and without it, guidance is not possible. Therefore, it is essential for all Muslims to make an effort to understand and study Hadith, even if it is at a basic level.

Unfortunately, most of the works of Hadith literature available in English are long, detailed, and viewed as heavy reads by the general masses. As these are religious texts, it can be daunting for beginners to understand the subject. There are mainly two types of books about Hadith in English. While one type deals with the science of Hadith in terms of its historical phenomena as a vital Islamic institution, the other consists of thick volumes of English renditions of Hadith corpuses—both of which can put off beginners from reading and understanding Hadith.

This dilemma gave birth to the 'Forty Ahadith' project, in which we set out to compile a series of forty ahadith from each of the six canonical books of Hadith. The collection aims to educate people who wish to enjoy Hadith literature without delving too deep into its technicalities. The style and language used in these books is non-specialised and thereby accessible to readers of all levels and ages. As such, the collection is also ideal for new Muslims who wish to learn more about Hadith.

In this particular volume, we have selected forty ahadith from *Sunan al-Nasā'ī* in order to give the reader a flavour of the Hadith literature found within the *Sunan*. There is no particular reason for choosing the ahadith mentioned herein. However, each hadith will reflect a unique theme so as to touch upon various aspects of the Islamic teachings, such as:

- Manners and Etiquettes
- Character of a Muslim
- Exhortations and Admonitions
- Remembrance of Allah
- Knowledge and Action
- Beliefs

When selecting the forty ahadith for each book in the series, we made sure to avoid lengthy and elaborate narrations or those that dealt with complex legal and theological matters. Instead, you will find that the selected ahadith focus on character, spirituality, morals, manners and ethics, and that the accompanying explanations of the ahadith focus on highlighting these aspects.

Within this volume is a simple discussion of the theoretical parameters of praiseworthy characters every Muslim should aspire to achieve, supererogatory virtuous acts of worship, and the moral philosophy (in particular normative ethics) of these ahadith. It is hoped that this will open the doors for readers to enquire more about Hadith as an important source of revelation.

Finally, it is worth pointing out that the reason for compiling forty ahadith is due to the virtuous nature of 'forty' ahadith recorded in many traditions of the Prophet Muhammad ﷺ. It is related that Prophet Muhammad ﷺ said, 'Whoever memorises forty ahadith regarding the matters of religion, Allah will resurrect him on the Day of Judgement from among the group of jurists and scholars' (*Bayhaqī*). Although this hadith is weak in its authenticity, many scholars have strongly supported acting on weak ahadith, which solely speak about virtues of good deeds, for the sake of spirituality. What is of even more benefit is to memorise forty ahadith from *Sunan al-Nasā'ī*. The short ahadith in this compilation may help facilitate young learners and beginners to memorise the beloved Prophet's sayings, which would be a great achievement.

We would like to conclude by thanking everyone who has made this project possible, especially Br Haris Ahmad from Kube Publishing House for his support; without his help, this project would not have been possible. The people we are most indebted to are the patrons of the Ibn Rushd Centre of Excellence for Islamic Research. This work is dedicated to them and all those who support the advancement of knowledge and research.

Shahrul Hussain & Zahed Fettah
8th April 2019 / 3rd Sha'bān 1440

Acknowledgments

It would not be possible to accomplish this work without the support of many great people, too many to mention all of them by name. First and foremost, we thank our parents for their love and support. Our teachers without whom we would be nothing. We are most obliged to mention our heartfelt thanks to Abida Akhtar and Sumayah Ali for their invaluable feedback. The English language or indeed any other language does not afford a word to express our deepest gratitude to Br Rizvan Khalid for his support and help.

I would like to thank Shaykh Fahimul Anam from Gift of Knowledge for his long standing support and friendship and Shaykh Abdullah Hasan from the British Board of Scholars and Imams for his commitment to serving knowledge and scholarship and for his friendship. Br Mohammed Nawaz, one of the most amazing personalities I have come across, willing to go out of his way to help good causes. May Allah bless him.

"I ask Allah to raise the rank of my parents and bless them in this life and the next, for they have encouraged me on my path of learning and seeking knowledge."

Zahed Fettah

A Brief Biography of Imam al-Nasā'ī

(Abū 'Abd al-Raḥmān) Aḥmad ibn Shu'ayb ibn 'Alī ibn Sīnān al-Nasā'ī, famously known as Imam al-Nasā'ī, was a genius in Hadith, possessing one of the most brilliant minds of Hadith scholarship in the history of Islam. He was born in the town of Nasa' in Khurasan in the year 215 AH. He sought knowledge from a young age, travelling to Qutaybah ibn Sa'īd in the year 230 AH when he was only around 15 years old. He spent just over a year narrating a lot of ahadith from him.

Many scholars have spoken highly of Imam al-Nasā'ī. Abū Aḥmad ibn 'Adi said: 'I heard Manṣūr and Abū Ja'far al-Ṭaḥāwī saying that Nasā'ī is from the imams for the Muslims.' Imam Ḥākim al-Naysābūrī related from Imam Dāraquṭnī that he said: 'Abū 'Abd al-Raḥmān (Nasā'ī) is above anyone else at his time when it comes to Hadith.' Dāraquṭnī also said, when he was asked about Imam al-Nasā'ī and Imam Ibn Khuzaymah: 'I do not prefer anyone over al-Nasā'ī, although Ibn Khuzaymah is an imam of exceptional accuracy and there is none like him.'

Imam Dāraquṭnī also said: 'Abū 'Abd al-Raḥmān al-Nasā'ī had the greatest knowledge of *fiqh* from amongst all the scholars of Egypt in his time. Alongside this, he had the greatest knowledge of authentic and weak hadith, and hadith narrators. When he reached such a high level, he was envied by others.'

Imam al-Nasā'ī was described as being a handsome man. He was known to be very pious and always engaging in the worship Allah. He would fast regularly and would only eat moderately.

Imam al-Nasā'ī authored a number of important books, including *Sunan al-Kubrā*, *Al-Mujtabā* (better known as *al-Sunan al-Ṣughrā*), and *'Amal al-Yawm wa al-Laylah*. The first of these books contains around 12,000 narrations of ahadith. This was then summarised in *al-Mujtabā* which contains just over 5,000 narrations and became known as *Sunan al-Nasā'ī*. This then became one of the five most important references of hadith, alongside *Ṣaḥīḥ al-Bukhārī*, *Ṣaḥīḥ Muslim*, *Sunan Abū Dāwūd*, and *Sunan al-Tirmidhī*. In his book, Imam al-Nasā'ī generally only reports authentic narrations, with the exception of few ahadith. Hence, his book was viewed by many scholars as being the most authentic of the six books of Hadith, after *Ṣaḥīḥ al-Bukhārī* and *Ṣaḥīḥ Muslim*.

Sunan al-Nasā'ī is arranged according to the chapters of law. The author placed chapter headings before he reported one hadith or more on a particular subject. These headings provide important insight into the legal positions of Imam al-Nasā'ī. He did not follow any of the four legal schools of jurisprudence but was an independent judge and jurist who had his own views. Sometimes, after reporting a hadith, the author comments on it, particularly if it contains a weakness or some sort of defect. This makes his great work an essential reference not only for Hadith scholars, but also for legal scholars.

Imam al-Nasā'ī passed away in the year 303 AH. There is historical disagreement about whether Imam al-Nasā'ī passed away in Makkah or in Palestine, may Allah have mercy on him.

The Importance of Hadith and its Significance

Allah sent Messengers throughout history with the objective of clarifying the truth to the people and guiding them to Him. Many of these Messengers were also sent with Books containing guidance, such as the final Messenger of Allah, Prophet Muhammad ﷺ. He was sent to teach the Book, the Qur'an, and to be the living example of the teachings of the Qur'an. As Allah states in the Qur'an: *'Allah has surely conferred a favour on the believers when He sent in their midst a Messenger from among themselves who recites to them His verses, purifies them, and teaches them the Book and the Wisdom, while previously they had been in clear misguidance'* (*Āl 'Imrān* 3: 164). Allah also states: *'And we have sent down the Reminder (the Qur'an) to you so that you (O Messenger) may clarify to the people that which has been sent down to them, and so that they may ponder'* (*al-Naḥl* 16: 44).

These verses highlight that the role of the Messenger ﷺ is to clarify and teach the Qur'an. His words and his actions, which form a verbal and practical interpretation of the Qur'an, is the Prophetic Tradition referred to as the 'Sunnah'. Following the Sunnah is necessary because it is the only way to practice the teachings of the final Book of Allah correctly.

Allah has taken it upon Himself to preserve the Qur'an: *'It is certainly We who have revealed the Reminder, and it is certainly We who will preserve it'* (*al-Ḥijr* 15: 9). This preservation is not restricted to the letters and words of the Qur'an but also includes the preservation of its meanings, which is fulfilled through the Prophetic implementation of the Qur'an—the Sunnah.

It is simply not possible to observe the teachings of Islam without following the Sunnah. The purpose of the Qur'an is to teach us the correct belief and acts of worship Allah demands from us in order to prove our servitude to Him. It is not, however, an instruction manual detailing precise rules and methods of worshipping Allah.

Moreover, written or verbal instructions are not enough; it requires a teacher to show us the practical way of worshipping Allah. Thus, while the Qur'an outlines the commandments of Allah such as to fast, give zakat, perform hajj and the like, the role of the Prophet ﷺ is to teach us *how* to perform those acts of worship. Therefore, without knowing and following the Sunnah, Muslims will not be able to observe the teachings of the Qur'an.

Compilation of Hadith

Although the Qur'an was collected and written in one place much earlier than the Hadith, the latter was also preserved in similar ways to the former. Ahadith were written down by some Companions at the time of the Messenger ﷺ, but this habit only became widespread a century or so after his death.

Since the second century after *hijrah*, many scholars wrote down the ahadith of the Prophet ﷺ. Some scholars compiled books of Hadith which discussed the various areas of the teachings of the Prophet ﷺ. Sadly, some of the earliest books of Hadith were lost. However, some survived and were transmitted throughout centuries until our time, including the *Muwaṭṭā'* of Imam Mālik (d. 179 AH), the *Muṣannaf* of 'Abd al-Razzāq (d. 211 AH), the *Muṣannaf* of Ibn Abī Shaybah (d. 235 AH), and the *Musnad* of Imam Aḥmad ibn Ḥanbal (d. 241 AH). These books contain thousands of reports from the Prophet ﷺ and his Companions, clarifying how they implemented the Qur'anic teachings in their everyday life.

Hundreds of books of Hadith were authored, but only a dozen of them became famous and spread worldwide. The nine most relied-upon books of Hadith are:

1. *Ṣaḥīḥ al-Bukhārī*
2. *Ṣaḥīḥ Muslim*
3. *Sunan Abū Dāwūd*
4. *Sunan al-Tirmidhī*
5. *Sunan al-Nasā'ī*
6. *Sunan Ibn Mājah*

7. *Muwaṭṭa' Mālik*
8. *Musnad Aḥmad*
9. *Musnad al- Dārimī*

The Classification of Hadith

In the early generations, during the time of the Companions of the Prophet, it was quite easy to know the Sunnah of the Prophet ﷺ because the Companions had witnessed him directly. Unfortunately, in the generations that followed, some people would make false attributions to the Prophet ﷺ and claim that he said things which he had not said. They would do this with different intentions and agendas. This led to the scholars of Hadith putting an impressive amount of effort into preserving the Sunnah and distinguishing between authentic reports and false ones. They would study chains of narrations, the biographies of hadith narrators, and the texts of hadith in order to conclude which reports can comfortably be attributed to the Prophet ﷺ. Volumes have been written about those who narrated hadith so that we are able to know who the reliable and unreliable transmitters of hadith are. This effort was a collective one by many of the greatest scholars of Hadith, ensuring that the Sunnah of the Prophet ﷺ was preserved so that the Muslims may act upon it as Allah commanded them in the Qur'an.

This effort to study the Prophetic Traditions resulted in the formation of the science of Hadith. This became one of the most important of the Islamic sciences. It discusses chains of narration, different types of ahadith, the conditions for an authentic hadith, the different methods of transmitting hadith, the *fiqh* (understanding) of ahadith, and other relevant areas. Separate books have been authored in this science, known as *uṣūl al-ḥadīth* or *muṣṭalaḥ al-ḥadīth*, from the fourth century onwards. Some prominent works in this field include, *Ma'rifat 'Ulūm al-Ḥadīth* by Ḥākim al-Naysābūrī (d. 405 AH) and *Ma'rifat Anwā' 'Ulūm al-Ḥadīth* by Imam Abū 'Amr ibn al-Ṣalāḥ (d. 643 AH).

Studying the sciences of Hadith is an essential part of Islamic studies. We can only understand the Qur'an and the Shariah if we have a strong grounding in the sciences of Hadith and a good understanding of the *fiqh* of Hadith.

However, Hadith studies is usually a subject for the most dedicated of learners because it requires attention to detail. For instance, there are many classifications and categories of Hadith. Advanced readers can refer to the *Muqaddimah* by Ibn Ṣalāḥ which is also available in English. Readers who have access to Arabic can refer to many resources such as *al-Irshād* by al-Nawawī (which he later summarised in his *Taqrīb*), al-Suyūṭī's *Tadrīb al-Rāwī,* Ibn Kathīr's *Ikhtiṣār 'Ulūm al-Ḥadīth*, al-Zarkashī's *al-Nukat,* al-'Iraqi's *al-Taqyīd wa al-Īḍāḥ* and Ibn Ḥajar al-'Asqalānī's *Nukhbat al-Fikr*.

As a beginner, you should know that scholars have made four major classifications of hadith based on the soundness of the hadith in terms of the reliability and memory of its reporters:

1. *Ṣaḥīḥ* (rigorously authentic)
2. *Ḥasan* (good)
3. *Ḍa'īf* (weak)
4. *Mawḍū'* (fabricated)

Ṣaḥīḥ (rigorously authentic)

This is defined by Ibn Ṣalāḥ as a hadith which has a continuous chain of narrators (*isnād*), who have narrated the hadith from only trustworthy (*thiqah*) narrators (those with perfect memory and uprightness) and it (the hadith) is free from irregularities (in the text) and defects (in the *isnād*). Such as: Mālik—from Nāfi'—from 'Abdullāh ibn Umar.

Ḥasan (good)

Al-Tirmidhī defines *ḥasan* as a hadith which is not irregular (*shādh*) nor contains a disparaged reporter in its chain of narrators, and is reported through more than one channel. Examples of *ḥasan* ahadith are those which have been reported by: 'Amr ibn Shu'ayb—from his father—from his grandfather or Muḥammad ibn 'Amr—from Abū Salamah—from Abū Hurayrah.

Ḍa'īf (weak)

A weak hadith is a hadith which has failed to meet the standard of *ṣaḥīḥ* or *ḥasan*. It is usually one that has faults in the continuity of the chain of narrators (*isnād*) or has a fault in a narrator in terms of lack of reliability either in memory or uprightness.

Mawḍū' (fabricated)

These are ahadith which the Prophet Muhammad ﷺ never said, but due to personal motives, were fabricated and attributed to him. A fabricated hadith can be detected either because one of the narrators is known to be a liar or because the text is of an obnoxious nature, thus going against the principles of Islam. For example, it is (falsely) attributed to the Prophet Muhammad ﷺ that he said, 'A negro will fornicate when his belly is full and steal when he is hungry.' This is fabricated due to its obnoxious nature, hence going against the noble character of the Prophet Muhammad ﷺ.

Oftentimes though, the wordings of a fabricated hadith may be non-offensive or even sound sensible. For example, 'To return one *dāniq* (a sixth of a dirham) to its owner is better than worshipping (Allah) for seventy years.' At such instances, scrutinising the hadith based on the thoroughly developed science of hadith classification would help us determine if it was in fact narrated by the Prophet Muhammad ﷺ or simply made up and falsely attributed to him.

1

Asking for Power and Authority

عَنْ عَبْدِ الرَّحْمَنِ بْنِ سَمُرَةَ قَالَ قَالَ رَسُولُ اللَّهِ ﷺ لاَ تَسْأَلِ الإِمَارَةَ فَإِنَّكَ إِنْ أُعْطِيتَهَا عَنْ مَسْأَلَةٍ وُكِلْتَ إِلَيْهَا وَإِنْ أُعْطِيتَهَا عَنْ غَيْرِ مَسْأَلَةٍ أُعِنْتَ عَلَيْهَا

It was narrated that 'Abd al-Raḥmān ibn Samurah ﵁ said: 'The Messenger of Allah ﷺ said: "Do not ask for leadership. For if it is given to you because of asking, you will be left to your own devices, but if it is given to you without asking, you will be helped (by Allah)."'

Allah has created humankind in a way that they need leadership to be able to function in an orderly fashion. Without leadership, human society would be in chaos and disorder. The significance of leadership can be seen in the verse in which Allah talks about the reason why he created Adam ﵇, *'And When Allah said to the angels, indeed I will create on Earth a vicegerent'* (*al-Baqarah* 2: 30). The purpose of Adam's creation was to serve as a leader and implement the laws of God on Earth. He was endowed by Allah with the authority to teach the law of Allah to his children.

Every Prophet taught his followers about leadership and the importance of following leadership. The Prophet Muhammad ﷺ was no exception. He extolled his followers about the virtues, importance and significance of leadership. It is reported that the Prophet Muhammad ﷺ said, 'The imam (leader) is but a shield from behind which the people fight and by which they protect themselves.' The Prophet Muhammad ﷺ instructed Muslims to choose a person who will provide leadership and make decisions even on the smallest level. For example, he instructed two people on a journey to appoint one of them to be the emir of the journey, and suggested that the eldest of the two be the leader. These ahadith show the importance and significance of leadership in Islam, to the extent that even in a situation of two people, one of them should be appointed as the emir to make decisions.

The point is not to have an emir just for the sake of it, but that the emir must be obeyed, even if you do not agree with him or his decisions. The instruction of the Prophet ﷺ is clear that the leader must be obeyed. If you are in a workplace and you do not agree with the decisions made by the leader, you can either discuss your issues with them or resign from that post, but you cannot actively work against the emir, unless they go against the laws of Allah and His Messenger ﷺ.

Although Islam explicitly teaches Muslims the importance of political leadership, this hadith teaches us that leadership should not be sought. It is un-Islamic for a person to ask others to put them in power or to crave for power. Rather, it should be that the people approach a person to ask them to assume the leadership post. This is because leadership comes with great responsibility. Hence, the vast majority of the Prophet's Companions did not pursue leadership posts.

Leaders will be asked by Allah on the Day of Judgement about how they ruled. Consider Abu Bakr's statement where he said that he would regard himself as responsible in front of Allah if a dog were to die of starvation during his reign. Such is the level of responsibility in leadership. In Islam, leaders are persuaded to accept the post when people see that person to be a good fit to lead them based on their track record of serving people and being committed to their service. If a person asks for power, then Allah will not help them; but on the other hand, a person who has been selected by the people to lead them will receive Allah's help. The only exception to this rule is if one believes that not taking up a leadership role may result in greater general harm. In this case, the person is excused because they are not seeing leadership for the sake of leadership, but instead to protect people from harm and to benefit them.

2

The Virtues of Converting to Islam

عَنْ أَبِى سَعِيدٍ الْخُدْرِيِّ قَالَ قَالَ رَسُولُ اللَّهِ ﷺ إِذَا أَسْلَمَ الْعَبْدُ
فَحَسُنَ إِسْلاَمُهُ كَتَبَ اللَّهُ لَهُ كُلَّ حَسَنَةٍ كَانَ أَزْلَفَهَا وَمُحِيَتْ عَنْهُ
كُلُّ سَيِّئَةٍ كَانَ أَزْلَفَهَا ثُمَّ كَانَ بَعْدَ ذَلِكَ الْقِصَاصُ الْحَسَنَةُ بِعَشْرَةِ
أَمْثَالِهَا إِلَى سَبْعِمِائَةِ ضِعْفٍ وَالسَّيِّئَةُ بِمِثْلِهَا إِلاَّ أَنْ يَتَجَاوَزَ اللَّهُ
عَزَّ وَجَلَّ عَنْهَا

It was narrated that Abū Sa'īd al-Khudrī ؓ said: 'The Messenger of Allah ﷺ said: "If a person accepts Islam, such that his Islam is good, Allah will decree reward for every good deed that he did before, and every bad deed that he did before will be erased. Then after that will come the reckoning; each good deed will be rewarded ten times up to seven hundred times. And each bad deed will be recorded as it is, unless Allah, the Mighty and Sublime, forgives it.'"

Unlike some religions which allow membership to only certain races or people of a certain community, Islam is a call to all of humanity with the message of worshipping only One God. We know from other ahadith that everyone is born with a pure and clean slate inclining to the worship of Allah. This is known as the *fitrah*. However, it is their parents or guardians who influence their religious beliefs which take them away from that purity. Allah created human beings to worship Him and gave them intelligence to work out what is right and what is wrong. Any wrong decisions a person makes is their responsibility and no one else can be blamed for it.

The Prophet Muhammad ﷺ came with the message of Islam to his people, the Arabs. At that time, the majority of Makkans used to worship idols. Through patience and perseverance, the Prophet Muhammad ﷺ taught people about Islam and taught them to worship only One God. Little by little people accepted Islam, but this was not without consequence. It is not easy for people to leave their faith and join another. There are massive implications, and it is one of the hardest things for people to do.

The early Muslims were subjected to brutal persecution, torture and harassment because they accepted Islam and chose to worship One God. Their families disowned them and cut them off from inheritance, help, shelter and food. It was this great sacrifice that Allah wanted to acknowledge by wiping out their previous sins and converting their good deeds into *thawāb* (spiritual rewards).

This hadith teaches us a few important lessons. Firstly, the good deeds of non-Muslims are not considered as *thawāb*. Their good deeds will be rewarded to them in this world only. Secondly, Allah wipes out all the sins someone committed before converting to Islam; no matter what it was they did, they will not face questioning for those sins on the Day of Judgement. Allah has promised such a person forgiveness. It is from the point of conversion to Islam that accountability (*ḥisāb*) starts. The Prophet Muhammad ﷺ tells us that good deeds are multiplied by anything between 10 to 700 units of *thawāb*. However, due to Allah's mercy, sin is written as a single-entry bad deed; it is not multiplied. The reward for good is permanent (unless someone does something to spoil it), but sins are easily forgiven by Allah.

3

The Things to Seek Refuge in Allah From

عَنْ عَمْرِو بْنِ مَيْمُونٍ الأَوْدِيِّ قَالَ كَانَ سَعْدٌ يُعَلِّمُ بَنِيهِ هَؤُلاَءِ الْكَلِمَاتِ كَمَا يُعَلِّمُ الْمُعَلِّمُ الْغِلْمَانَ وَيَقُولُ إِنَّ رَسُولَ اللَّهِ ﷺ كَانَ يَتَعَوَّذُ بِهِنَّ دُبُرَ الصَّلاَةِ اللَّهُمَّ إِنِّي أَعُوذُ بِكَ مِنَ الْبُخْلِ وَأَعُوذُ بِكَ مِنَ الْجُبْنِ وَأَعُوذُ بِكَ أَنْ أُرَدَّ إِلَى أَرْذَلِ الْعُمُرِ وَأَعُوذُ بِكَ مِنْ فِتْنَةِ الدُّنْيَا وَأَعُوذُ بِكَ مِنْ عَذَابِ الْقَبْرِ

It was narrated that ʿAmr ibn Maymūn al-Awdī said: ʿSaʿd used to teach his children these words as a teacher teaches his young students, and he said that the Messenger of Allah ﷺ used to seek refuge by means of them at the end of every prayer: "O Allah, I seek refuge in You from miserliness, and I seek refuge in You from cowardice, and I seek refuge in You from reaching the age of senility, and I seek refuge in You from the trials of this world, and I seek refuge in You from the torment of the grave.'"

The physical movements of the five daily prayers are only one aspect of this great act of worship. The icing on the cake, so to speak, is a person making supplication (*du'ā'*) to Allah after the prayer. Making supplications to Allah has been extolled so much by the Prophet Muhammad ﷺ and commanded by Allah in the Qur'an. Allah reassures us that He hears every prayer of every caller and that He responds to our prayers.

Not all our prayers will be granted, but all our prayers will be heard by Allah and He will personally reply back to our calls. This is a real honour in itself so we should seize every opportunity to make *du'ā'* to Allah. If we write or phone a famous person and they write back to us, we feel so honoured and happy; then imagine how much more honoured we should feel when Allah replies back to us!

One of the best times to make supplication to Allah is after prayer, and this was done by the Prophet Muhammad ﷺ himself. There were several things he would pray for, but he wanted to teach us important things we may not have thought about.

After every prayer, the Prophet Muhammad ﷺ used to read this supplication:

Allāhumma innī a'ūdhu bika minal-bukhli, wa a'ūdhu bika minal-jubni, wa a'ūdhu bika an uradda ilā ardhalil-'umurī, wa a'ūdhu bika min fitnatid-dunyā, wa a'ūdhu bika min 'adhābil-qabr

The Prophet ﷺ asked Allah to protect him from five things: miserliness, cowardice, reaching the age of senility, the trials of this world and the torment of the grave.

There are two traits most despicable for a person to have; they are miserliness and cowardice, and they are usually symptoms of one another. A lot can be achieved if everyone contributed to building a better society for everyone to enjoy. There are some who do not want to spend and give to charitable causes such as building schools, universities, play centres for children, libraries and the like, but they are happy to benefit from them. Why is it that only a few people give to these causes? When everyone has the capacity to give *something*, they must give what they can. But some people are unwilling to do so, because they suffer from stinginess. For them, holding on to the money they have is their greatest objective. They fear that their money will decrease, and they will lose out on their wealth, whereas Allah and His Messenger ﷺ have promised them that their money will be returned to them. They lack certainty of this fact and rely only on what they can physically see, which is a decrease in money.

Cowardice does not only imply fear of fighting in wars, but can also translate to a fear of standing up and challenging tyranny from rulers or anyone in authority. Ignoring injustice and not speaking out against it due to fear is also a form of cowardice.

In the supplication, the Prophet ﷺ also asked Allah for protection from reaching a very advanced age, when a person cannot remember basic things and becomes completely dependent on others. This is because there is dignity in being able to clean oneself after using the toilet, bathing oneself, and being able to move by oneself. When people become dependent regarding these basic things, everyone starts to see them as a burden and people start to get fed up of them. This harms the dignity of a person and so, the Prophet ﷺ taught us to ask Allah not to grant us such an ending in life.

Facing trials in this life tests a person's faith. Humans are weak, and at times of disaster it is quite easy for many of us to lose our faith. While tests are placed in our lives to make us spiritually stronger, they could lead to the exact opposite if we let them. The biggest damage we could do to ourselves is to let trials and tests bring our faith down. Having said that, it is only natural to get adversely affected during times of distress. There is nothing abnormal or blameworthy about it, and no one is immune to feeling low levels of faith. But it becomes dangerous when our spirituality dips so low that it risks our faith altogether. It was for this reason that the Prophet Muhammad ﷺ sought protection from the trials of this world.

The Prophet Muhammad ﷺ also taught us to seek refuge from the punishment of the grave. The punishment of the grave is extremely severe, and if a person faces torment in there, their reckoning in front of Allah will be hard, but if their experience in the grave is easy then their reckoning will also be easy. This is why the Prophet Muhammad ﷺ would seek protection from the punishment of the grave before the punishment of Hell.

This supplication is profound in that it is comprehensive and seeks protection from things we wouldn't have thought twice about. It is important that we follow the Prophet Muhammad ﷺ in memorising and reciting this supplication to live a wholesome life in both worlds.

Hygiene: Washing Hands before Dipping them into the Water Vessel

عَنْ أَبِي هُرَيْرَةَ أَنَّ النَّبِيَّ ﷺ قَالَ إِذَا اسْتَيْقَظَ أَحَدُكُمْ مِنْ نَوْمِهِ فَلاَ يَغْمِسْ يَدَهُ فِي وَضُوبِهِ حَتَّى يَغْسِلَهَا ثَلاَثًا فَإِنَّ أَحَدَكُمْ لاَ يَدْرِى أَيْنَ بَاتَتْ يَدُه

It was narrated from Abū Hurayrah ﷺ that the Prophet ﷺ said: 'When any one of you wakes from sleep, let him not dip his hand in (the water he uses for) his ablution until he has washed it three times, for none of you knows where his hand spent the night.'

Personal hygiene should be an important part of our lives. It protects us against many viruses and illnesses. Lack of personal hygiene is something most people find disgusting and repulsive. The Prophet ﷺ has encouraged us to regularly wash ourselves and more so during public gatherings such as the Friday prayers and the Eid prayers. Safeguarding against urine and faeces was equally emphasised, because purification is considered to be a part of faith. Complete faith is not achieved by people who fail to maintain purity, cleanliness and personal hygiene.

Sometimes, people forget or do not realise that the action they are about to perform may cause contamination and spread disease, or at the least, that people would find it unpleasant. A common way of spreading viruses is by our hands. This is because it is the part of the body most used to do things with in our lives. Therefore, keeping our hands clean is essential.

During sleep, the body is unaware of what it is doing. If any part of our body itches while we are asleep, our brain automatically dictates our hand to scratch that area. Because we do not know where our hands have been, it is important to wash them before immersing them into clean water so as to avoid contaminating it with impurities and possible diseases.

This hadith teaches us the importance of personal hygiene, to be vigilant about keeping ourselves clean, and washing our hands between two acts. Washing hands after using the toilet, washing hands before preparing food, and washing hands after sweeping the floor are but a few examples of when we ought to be washing our hands. It is worth remembering that without maintaining purity, cleanliness, and personal hygiene, complete faith in Islam cannot be achieved.

5

Virtues of Voluntary Worship (Nawāfil)

عَنْ أَبِي هُرَيْرَةَ أَنَّ النَّبِيَّ ﷺ قَالَ إِنَّ أَوَّلَ مَا يُحَاسَبُ بِهِ الْعَبْدُ يَوْمَ الْقِيَامَةِ صَلاَتُهُ فَإِنْ وُجِدَتْ تَامَّةً كُتِبَتْ تَامَّةً وَإِنْ كَانَ انْتَقَصَ مِنْهَا شَيْءٌ قَالَ انْظُرُوا هَلْ تَجِدُونَ لَهُ مِنْ تَطَوُّعٍ يُكَمِّلُ لَهُ مَا ضَيَّعَ مِنْ فَرِيضَةٍ ثُمَّ سَائِرُ الأَعْمَالِ تَجْرِي عَلَى حَسَبِ ذَلِكَ

It was narrated from Abū Hurayrah رضي الله عنه that the Prophet ﷺ said: 'The first thing for which a person will be brought to account on the Day of Resurrection will be his *ṣalāh*. If it is found to be complete then it will be recorded as complete, and if anything is lacking Allah will say: "Look and see if you can find any voluntary prayers with which to complete what he neglected of his obligatory prayers." Then the rest of his deeds will be reckoned in like manner.'

Allah created human beings to worship Him. As such He fixed for them certain acts of worship they must complete. The five daily prayers, fasting the month of Ramadan, paying zakat and performing hajj are examples of acts of worship Muslims must observe as their commitment to Islam. In return for their obedience, Allah will grant them Paradise and everlasting happiness. From the four major acts of worship, prayer is the only one which is performed regularly and daily. The other acts of worship are required only once a year and even then, they are only due if the conditions are met. For example, hajj and zakat are only obligatory if a person can afford it. Therefore, it may be that a person may never be able to observe these two acts of worship in their lives. Fasting is only obligatory if someone is physically able to fast, and therefore some people may not be able to fast their entire life or many years of it. Prayer, on the other hand, is different. It does not have conditions of affordability, wealth or health. If a person is unable to stand, then they can sit and pray, and if they cannot sit and pray then they can lie down and pray. Prayer in all circumstances is required and no exception is made.

Prayer stands as the most important of the pillars of Islam after the *shahādah*, and therefore it should be no surprise that it is the first thing for which Allah will hold us accountable. There are two things to remark from this. Firstly, the importance of prayer; in the sense that before you are asked about anything else you have done, prayer will be the first thing you are questioned about. Secondly, if a person's prayer is correctly accounted for, then the rest of their reckoning will be easy, but if the reckoning for prayer is bad then what will follow will be worse.

The mercy and love of Allah for His creation is so much that He has provided many opportunities for us to seek redemption and forgiveness. Allah has sent the Prophet Muhammad ﷺ as a guide and commanded Muslims to follow him. For almost every compulsory act of worship, the Prophet Muhammad ﷺ would add some extra acts of worship in order to make it a complete package, so to speak. These extra acts of worship are known as *nawāfil*. The *nawāfil* carry with them great reward and help a person to get closer to Allah and earn His favour. There is another great benefit of observing the *nawāfil* acts of worship which this hadith talks about. It is that when there are deficiencies in the *farḍ* or compulsory acts of worship, Allah will instruct the angels to see if that person has performed any voluntary acts of worship. If they have, then those acts of worship will be used to make up for any shortcomings in the obligatory actions. The same will be applied for all other acts of *farḍ* worship.

This hadith aims to encourage Muslims to engage in as much *nawāfil* prayers and acts of worship as possible. It has become a habit for many to just offer their *farḍ* prayers and neglect the Sunnah prayers. However, it is important to offer the *nawāfil* in order to get closer to Allah and for it to act as a means of making up the shortcomings in our worship of Allah.

Just About Catching the Prayer

عَنْ أَبِي هُرَيْرَةَ ﵁ عَنِ النَّبِيِّ ﷺ قَالَ مَنْ أَدْرَكَ رَكْعَةً مِنْ صَلاَةِ الْعَصْرِ قَبْلَ أَنْ تَغْرُبَ الشَّمْسُ أَوْ رَكْعَةً مِنْ صَلاَةِ الصُّبْحِ قَبْلَ أَنْ تَطْلُعَ الشَّمْسُ فَقَدْ أَدْرَكَ

It was narrated from Abū Hurayrah ﵁ that the Prophet ﷺ said: 'Whoever catches up with one *rak'ah* (unit) of 'Aṣr prayer before the sun sets, or one *rak'ah* of the Fajr prayer before the sun rises, has caught it.'

Allah has made the five daily prayers compulsory on every Muslim to perform. These prayers do not take a long time to offer, and they are spread out during the day at five crucial times to remind us about Allah and our duty towards Him. This constant reminder is there to help us remember the Oneness of Allah, the purpose of our creation, and that we will return to Allah after our death for reckoning. Not only has Allah made prayer compulsory, but He has made it compulsory during particular times and it must be offered within the allocated time. If it is not offered within that time, then the prayer becomes *qaḍā*. This means that it is considered a missed prayer. We should note that there must be a reason for having missed the prayer. If a person has no valid excuse for missing it, then they are considered sinful; but if they have an excuse, such as being asleep or having forgotten about it, then they are to make up the prayer and it is hoped that Allah will forgive them.

Human life is seldom without its challenges and it is inevitable that sometimes people will become very busy, so busy that prayer will be pushed back to the very end of its time. There is a warning about praying at the very last moment. The Prophet ﷺ described it as the prayer of a hypocrite, who delays his prayer to the very last moment and then rushes prayer and fails to remember Allah as he ought to. However, if there is a valid reason and it does not become a habit due to laziness, then there is no problem.

This hadith teaches us the absolute final time to offer prayer before the time expires. Although part of the prayer would be considered *qaḍā* if a person manages to offer just one unit (*rak'ah*) of the 'Aṣr prayer before the sun sets, Allah's mercy informs us that He will accept it as a prayer offered on time. This is an act of great kindness by Him. Allah seeks to make rules easy for us and when we make mistakes, He is most willing to forgive us.

The Forbidden Times to Pray

عَنْ مُوسَى بْنِ عُلَيٍّ عَنْ أَبِيهِ قَالَ سَمِعْتُ عُقْبَةَ بْنَ عَامِرٍ يَقُولُ ثَلاَثُ سَاعَاتٍ كَانَ رَسُولُ اللَّهِ ﷺ يَنْهَانَا أَنْ نُصَلِّيَ فِيهِنَّ أَوْ نَقْبُرَ فِيهِنَّ مَوْتَانَا حِينَ تَطْلُعُ الشَّمْسُ بَازِغَةً حَتَّى تَرْتَفِعَ وَحِينَ يَقُومُ قَائِمُ الظَّهِيرَةِ حَتَّى تَمِيلَ وَحِينَ تَضَيَّفُ لِلْغُرُوبِ حَتَّى تَغْرُبَ

It was narrated from Mūsā ibn 'Alī that his father said: 'I heard 'Uqbah ibn 'Āmir ﵁ say: "There are three times during which the Messenger of Allah ﷺ forbade us from praying or burying our dead: When the sun had clearly started to rise until it was fully risen; when it was directly overhead at noon until it had passed the zenith; and when it was close to setting until it had fully set."'

Human life consists of following instructions. It does not matter where you are, there will always be certain things you can do and certain things you cannot do. The worship of Allah is no exception to this. All acts of worship, no matter what it is, have rules. In fact, the more complicated the act of worship is, the more rules it has. One of the greatest acts of worship is *ṣalāh* (prayer), and that too has rules. *Ṣalāh* cannot be offered in any way and any manner we wish. There are rules and procedures which must be followed. Failing to observe them means that the prayer is not valid or that it is deficient. Prayers must be taken seriously and must be observed as the Prophet ﷺ taught us so that it is accepted by Allah and so that we worship Him in an informed and guided way.

The five daily prayers have fixed times in which they are to be offered. Whereas, general voluntary prayers can be offered at any time and are not restricted to particular times. For example, a person cannot offer the Ẓuhr prayer until the time for it starts. This is not the case for voluntary prayers, which can be offered at any time. However, this hadith teaches Muslims that there are certain times in the day in which voluntary prayers should not be performed. A person wishing to pray must wait for those times to pass and only after that may they engage in prayer.

The first of the three forbidden times is when the sun has clearly started to rise until it has fully risen. This is talking about the time of the Fajr prayer which starts when the sun rays hit the horizon. This indicates that the sun is in the process of rising and daytime is soon to appear clearly. The sun completely rising marks the end of that period and now all types of prayer can be offered.

The second prohibited time for prayer is when the sun is directly overhead at noon until it has passed the zenith. This is at midday. It marks the time when the sun has reached the height of its climb and ends when the sun tilts and comes to a stop. This tilting-decline takes a few minutes. After the sun declines from the meridian, the time for Ẓuhr starts.

The final prohibited time for prayer is when the sun is close to setting until it has fully set. When the sun is starting to set marks the end of the 'Aṣr time and the setting of the sun marks the start of the Maghrib prayer. Once the sun has set, people may offer their prayers once again.

The exception to this rule, in all three cases, is obligatory prayers that have been delayed. Most scholars allow for them to be prayed even at these times.

This hadith teaches us that voluntary prayers of any type are not allowed during these three periods of time. This rule also applies to the funeral prayer. What the Prophet ﷺ meant by 'burying the dead' in the hadith, was the prayer and not the actual act of burial.

8

Building Grand Mosques: A Sign of the Day of Judgement

عَنْ أَنَسٍ أَنَّ النَّبِيَّ ﷺ قَالَ مِنْ أَشْرَاطِ السَّاعَةِ أَنْ يَتَبَاهَى النَّاسُ فِي الْمَسَاجِدِ

It was narrated from Anas ﵁ that the Prophet ﷺ said: 'One of the signs of the Hour will be that people will show off in building *masjids*.'

The holiest buildings on Earth are the places designated for the worship of Allah. These places are called mosques or *masājid* in Arabic. The first house designated for the worship of Allah is the Kaaba in Makkah. Allah says in the Qur'an: *'Indeed the first House appointed for humankind to worship was at Makkah'* (*Āl 'Imrān* 3: 96).

There are special rules to help reinforce the sanctity of mosques, the most important of them being maintaining the purity of the mosque and that none other than Allah is worshiped therein. There are plenty of ahadith that talk about the virtues of mosques such as spending time in them, cleaning them, and the like. One particular virtue related to mosques is building them. The Prophet Muhammad ﷺ told us, 'Whoever builds a mosque, Allah will build for him a house in Paradise.'[1] The virtues of building a mosque also carry with it the reward for all the people using the mosque, those who benefit from it, the education that takes place in it, the refuge people take in it, and the guidance people receive through it—*all* this reward goes to the people who helped build it. Allah rewards those who use the mosque and those who build it.

It is important for Muslims wherever they may be to build mosques. Without it, Muslims will have no place to pray or provide religious education for their children. The mosque represents the hub of a community. It should be the place where Muslims access information, help, support, and resolve religious matters. Without a mosque in the community, Muslims are in serious peril.

This hadith is a fascinating one. It talks about the signs of the Day of Judgement. There is no doubt that the world will come to an end, but the exact time and date of that event is only known to Allah. However, Allah has disclosed some of the events that will take place before the world ends, in order to help us prepare for it. These signs exist so people can see with their own eyes the truth of the Prophet Muhammad's message. The prophethood of Muhammad ﷺ marked the first major sign of the end of times. All other events will follow like pearls falling in sequence from a broken necklace.

There are many signs of the Day of Judgement which the Prophet Muhammad ﷺ foretold over 1400 years ago, and we are living at a time when we can see many of them unfolding before our very eyes. One such event is the building of mosques to satisfy egos and in

1 Al-Bukhari, *Sahih al-Bukhari*, Hadith no. 1450

competition with others who have built grand mosques. The increase of wealth means that there is a pursuit to leave a legacy, a pursuit to build mega mosques not for the sake of catering to the needs of people, but in competition with others. Perhaps the Middle East can be taken as an example where we can see mega mosques being built and named after a person, only to create a race for others to copy and outdo that mosque. Soon these mosques will become tourist sites rather than places of guidance and worship. The amount of money spent decorating these mosques is heart-wrenching and one is forced to ask whether it is really worth decorating these mosques with actual gold and extravagant chandeliers.

We mustn't question a person's intention behind building mosques, because only Allah knows their true intentions, but it is certainly worrying to see this trend unfolding in front of our eyes. It is far more important to spend that money on ensuring that our mosques have an impact in our communities, such as paying competent imams and teachers to educate the people.

9

The Construction History of the Three Sacred Mosques

عَنْ إِبْرَاهِيمَ قَالَ كُنْتُ أَقْرَأُ عَلَى أَبِي الْقُرْآنَ فِي السِّكَّةِ فَإِذَا قَرَأْتُ السَّجْدَةَ سَجَدَ فَقُلْتُ يَا أَبَتِ أَتَسْجُدُ فِي الطَّرِيقِ فَقَالَ إِنِّي سَمِعْتُ أَبَا ذَرٍّ يَقُولُ سَأَلْتُ رَسُولَ اللَّهِ ﷺ أَيُّ مَسْجِدٍ وُضِعَ أَوَّلاً قَالَ الْمَسْجِدُ الْحَرَامُ قُلْتُ ثُمَّ أَيٌّ قَالَ الْمَسْجِدُ الأَقْصَى قُلْتُ وَكَمْ بَيْنَهُمَا قَالَ أَرْبَعُونَ عَامًا وَالأَرْضُ لَكَ مَسْجِدٌ فَحَيْثُمَا أَدْرَكْتَ الصَّلاَةَ فَصَلِّ

It was narrated that Ibrāhīm [ibn Yazīd al-Taymī] said: 'I used to recite Qur'an to my father on the road, and if I recited a verse in which prostration was required, he would prostrate. I said: O my father, do you prostrate on the street? He said: "I heard Abū Dharr ﵁ say: 'I asked the Messenger of Allah ﷺ: "Which mosque was built first?" He said: "Al-Masjid al-Ḥaram." I said: Then which? He said: "Al-Masjid al-Aqṣā." I said: How long was there between them? He said: "Forty years. And the earth is a *masjid* (a place of prostration) for you, so wherever you are when the time for prayer comes, pray."""'

This hadith provides us with some valuable information. Firstly, there are fourteen places in the Qur'an where Allah commands the Muslims to prostrate. Once a person recites any of these verses they should pause, stand and drop in prostration to Allah. This is called *sajdah al-tilāwah*. Abū Ḥanīfah was of the opinion that *sajdah al-tilāwah* is obligatory (*wājib*), whereas the other three great Imams argued that it was only recommended (Sunnah).

The second important piece of information this hadith gives us is that it confirms what is stated in the Qur'an—that the first place of worship made for humankind to worship Allah was the Kaaba in Makkah. This shows the importance of the Kaaba, not only to Muslims, but to the entire human species. It shows how special the Kaaba is to Allah as it represents His symbol for humankind as a place of gathering, sacredness, worship and peace. The second place Allah made as His place of worship is al-Masjid al-Aqṣā in Jerusalem.

An important piece of information is given to us about the building of the two mosques in terms of the time between them. The Prophet Muhammad ﷺ told us that the gap between the construction of the two mosques was forty years.

Who built the Kaaba and al-Masjid al-Aqṣā is also a subject of disagreement amongst scholars. Some scholars say the first person to build the Kaaba was Adam ﷺ and others say it was the angels. There is also the view that the Prophet Ibrāhīm and his son Ismā'īl ﷺ were the first to build it. The stronger view suggests that Prophet

Ibrāhīm and his son *rebuilt* the Kaaba and that it was built before them. However, there is no clear-cut evidence to affirm who was the first to build it. Although the timeline has historical value, it is really not significant in religious terms. What is significant is that the virtue of praying at these two mosques is enormous and everyone who is able to pray in these mosques should seize the opportunity to do so.

The final lesson this hadith teaches us is that the entire earth is a place suitable for prayer. Although mosques are identified as sacred spaces for specific worship, a Muslim may pray wherever they are, whenever the prayer time starts. The only condition is that the place where they are praying must be pure and free from filth such as urine, stool, blood, alcohol, vomit and the like.

10

Superstition in Islam

عَنْ عَبْدِ اللَّهِ بْنِ عُمَرَ عَنْ رَسُولِ اللَّهِ ﷺ قَالَ إِنَّ الشَّمْسَ وَالْقَمَرَ لاَ يَخْسِفَانِ لِمَوْتِ أَحَدٍ وَلاَ لِحَيَاتِهِ وَلَكِنَّهُمَا آيَتَانِ مِنْ آيَاتِ اللَّهِ تَعَالَى فَإِذَا رَأَيْتُمُوهُمَا فَصَلُّوا

It was narrated from 'Abdullāh ibn Umar ﷺ that the Messenger of Allah ﷺ said: 'The sun and moon do not become eclipsed due to the death or birth of anyone; rather they are two of the signs of Allah the Most High. So when you see that then pray.'

Allah is the Creator of everything. He is All-Powerful and Almighty. Islam teaches us that everything happens by the will of Allah and nothing can happen without His will and command. In other words, things do not happen by accident; rather they occur because Allah wills for them to occur. Allah has created humankind as curious and rational creatures. As such, they want a logical explanation for things that happen. However, the occurrence of some things do not have a logical explanation that can be comprehended by humans. Because humans seek logical explanations, when they fail to find a logical explanation for something, they are unsettled and seek an answer that could explain that event.

The inability to submit to Allah's will and not pursue an explanation for something that cannot be explained leads to ascribing other circumstantial events as an explanation of the incident that they have found themselves to be in. This is what gives birth to superstitions. Throughout history, every culture and country has developed their own set of superstitious beliefs. For example, some people believe that walking under a ladder will bring bad luck or opening an umbrella indoors will bring about misfortune. Others say that a black cat passing by or a broken mirror bring about bad luck. In some parts of the world, people believe that if someone's palms itch, then wealth and money is imminent, whereas if the sole of the foot itches, then misfortune is on its way. These are nothing but empty statements people make to explain surprising events and link them to other events.

Islam tells Muslims to put their faith in Allah, even if they do not fully understand the event that has taken place. Everything happens because of the will of Allah. The story of Prophet Ya'qūb ﷺ illustrates this when he told his sons not to enter through one door, rather through different doors. Allah says in response to what Prophet Ya'qūb ﷺ said, *'This has no benefit in the least against (the will of Allah) but it was something Ya'qūb said from himself'* (*Yūsuf* 12: 68).

In some societies, superstition is exploited to advance personal gain. It is documented in history that some religious authorities used supernatural events to hold on to power and control people. For example, a shaman was believed to be a religious person in some societies, and it was believed that they achieve various powers through a trance or ecstatic religious experience. Shamans were typically thought to have the ability to heal the sick, to communicate with the 'otherworld', and often to escort the souls of the dead to that otherworld. In order to hold on to their status as revered people they would pretend to explain natural events like the eclipse in a way so as to advance their grip on people's emotions.

Now let us look at the example of the Prophet Muhammad ﷺ. When the Prophet Muhammad ﷺ was slightly senior in age, Allah blessed him with a son whom he named Ibrāhīm. Ibrāhīm did not survive and passed away a few months later. On the day Ibrāhīm passed away, there was an eclipse and so the Prophet's Companions came to him and said that even the sun and moon mourn the death of Ibrāhīm. Had he been dishonest and a fraud, the Prophet Muhammad ﷺ would have agreed with them because this was the perfect opportunity for him to strengthen his claim to prophethood. Instead, the Prophet ﷺ rejected any thought of the eclipse being connected to the death of his son Ibrāhīm. He taught his Companions that the sun and moon do not become eclipsed for the death or birth of anyone, rather they are two amazing signs of Allah and they do not respond to human emotions. He instructed them that the best thing they can do is to pray a two-unit prayer and ask for Allah's mercy and forgiveness.

11

Wishing for Death

عَنْ أَنَسٍ قَالَ قَالَ رَسُولُ اللَّهِ ﷺ أَلاَ لاَ يَتَمَنَّى أَحَدُكُمُ الْمَوْتَ لِضُرٍّ نَزَلَ بِهِ فَإِنْ كَانَ لاَ بُدَّ مُتَمَنِّيًا الْمَوْتَ فَلْيَقُلِ اللَّهُمَّ أَحْيِنِي مَا كَانَتِ الْحَيَاةُ خَيْرًا لِي وَتَوَفَّنِي إِذَا كَانَتِ الْوَفَاةُ خَيْرًا لِي

It was narrated that Anas ﵁ said: 'The Messenger of Allah ﷺ said: "None of you should wish for death because of some harm that befalls him. If he must wish for death, let him say: O Allah, keep me alive so long as life is good for me, and cause me to die when death is good for me."'

A common trait of human frailty is being impatient. Being patient is sometimes easier said than done, because it is in human nature to want things to be done instantly. Humans easily get stressed, anxious and worried and that is why we wish things to be done immediately. If someone has wronged us, we seek retaliation instantly, if we invest money in a business, we wish to become rich instantly.

Due to this human frailty, we struggle to deal with pain. There is no sort of pain which humans like or can endure. When pain hits, there is only one thing on the mind of the afflicted person and that is relief from that pain. We wait impatiently for the medicine to start its effect and some even overdose in the hope of trying to curtail their pain.

Human life is short, and it will come to an end one day or another. There is no doubt about that. The last days of life can be distressing and painful especially if someone is dying due to an illness or injury. Death is inevitable and will come to everyone. Although everyone wishes to live a long life, there can be circumstances when life becomes unbearable. It is difficult for the person enduring the hardship of life and pain to cope with this; and this also can take a toll on the life of those around the ailing person. They do not like to see the person in extreme anguish and pain, so euthanasia seems to be a popular recourse for many in the Western world as a solution to long-term incurable illness.

In this hadith, the Prophet ﷺ teaches Muslims that it is impermissible to ask for death or seek death. Death is the right of Allah and He will choose it for you. For a person to seek the means of ending their life is considered as entering a domain not befitting their station. Instead, the Prophet Muhammad ﷺ taught Muslims to ask Allah to do what is best for them. This is a lesson on *tawakkul* or putting faith in Allah to do what is best for us. The Prophet ﷺ taught Muslims who find themselves in the unfortunate state of incurable illness or some other prolonged pain to ask Allah:

Allāhumma aḥyinī mā kānatil-ḥayātu khairan-lī wa tawaffanī idhā kānatil-wafātu khairan-lī

"O Allah, keep me alive so long as life is good for me, and cause me to die when death is good for me"

This is the best thing to do, because it does not involve wishing for death, but instead reminds us to leave our affairs to Allah and to be content with whatever He decides for us. It is worth noting that every day a person spends in hardship, it is hoped that Allah will forgive them and expiate their sins. No hardship or calamity befalls a Muslim expect that Allah forgives some of his or her sins.

12

Funeral Prayer in Absentia

عن أَبِى سَلَمَةَ وَابْنِ الْمُسَيَّبِ أَنَّ أَبَا هُرَيْرَةَ أَخْبَرَهُمَا أَنَّ رَسُولَ اللّٰهِ ﷺ نَعَى لَهُمُ النَّجَاشِىَّ صَاحِبَ الْحَبَشَةِ الْيَوْمَ الَّذِى مَاتَ فِيهِ وَقَالَ اسْتَغْفِرُوا لأَخِيكُمْ

Abū Salamah and Ibn al-Musayyab narrated that Abū Hurayrah ﵁ told them that the Messenger of Allah ﷺ had told them of the death of al-Najāshī, the ruler of Abyssinia, on the day that he died, and he said: 'Pray for forgiveness for your brother.'

When the Prophet Muhammad ﷺ started to tell people about Islam, the Makkans felt threatened and so they started to attack the Muslims. They launched a campaign of abuse, torture and persecution with the aim of trying to stop Islam from spreading. The weakest in the community were subjected to the most abuse. They felt that their lives were at danger and risk, and they lived in constant fear. When things became unbearable, they came to the Prophet Muhammad ﷺ asking him for advice on what to do. The Prophet ﷺ suggested migrating to Abyssinia, a region near Ethiopia, because there lived a just king who did not oppress anyone, who was known as al-Najāshī. The Prophet ﷺ reassured the Companions that they will find safety and security there. So, in secrecy, some of the Muslims planned their flight from Makkah to Abyssinia. The non-Muslim leaders of Makkah tried to get the Muslims back but al-Najāshī refused to send them back and granted the Muslims a sanctuary and protection from any harm.

During a time when there was no one to help the Muslims, this man stepped up. He did not fear any consequence of harming commercial ties and friendship he had with the Makkans, and stuck up for the Muslims. It is worth noting that Muslims lived in Abyssinia for well over a decade, and although they were safe, they must have felt homesick. They sacrificed their desires for the sake of Allah and His religion. It was during the time of the Treaty of al-Ḥudaybiyyah that the Prophet ﷺ sent two boats to get them back home.

Al-Najāshī was a good man, a man who sought the truth. He was originally a Christian who converted to Islam, because he found the truth in Islam. It's interesting that al-Najāshī never met the Prophet Muhammad ﷺ, but when the Prophet ﷺ heard of his death he was saddened and asked people to pray for him. The Prophet ﷺ did his part by offering the funeral prayer in absentia. This is known as *al-Ṣalātu 'alā al-Ghā'ib.*

There is disagreement among the scholars as to whether *al-Ṣalātu 'alā al-Ghā'ib* is still an active Sunnah or not. Imam Abū Ḥanīfah, for example, did not believe it was. He argued that *al-Ṣalātu 'alā al-Ghā'ib* was only specific for the Prophet Muhammad ﷺ and not for others. The other three Imams, Mālik, Shāfi'ī and Aḥmad considered it as an active Sunnah and not particular to the Prophet Muhammad ﷺ.

They argued that there is no evidence suggesting *al-Ṣalātu 'alā al-Ghā'ib* to be specific to the Prophet Muhammad ﷺ. The default rule is that all the actions of the Prophet ﷺ are also to be applied by his followers, unless a clear proof exists to restrict it to him.

Al-Ṣalātu 'alā al-Ghā'ib is something every Muslim can do when someone has passed away, especially an important person such as a scholar. It is an opportunity to pray for the dead and pay our respects to them. Usually, people perform this prayer when someone notable has passed away in recognition of his or her contribution to the community.

13

When Does the Month of Ramadan Start?

عَنِ ابْنِ عَبَّاسٍ قَالَ عَجِبْتُ مِمَّنْ يَتَقَدَّمُ الشَّهْرَ وَقَدْ قَالَ رَسُولُ اللَّهِ ﷺ إِذَا رَأَيْتُمُ الْهِلاَلَ فَصُومُوا وَإِذَا رَأَيْتُمُوهُ فَأَفْطِرُوا فَإِنْ غُمَّ عَلَيْكُمْ فَأَكْمِلُوا الْعِدَّةَ ثَلاَثِينَ

It was narrated that Ibn 'Abbās ﵄ said: 'I am surprised at those who anticipate (are too eager to start) the month, when the Messenger of Allah ﷺ said: "When you see the new crescent then fast, and when you see it, then stop fasting, and if it is obscured from you (too cloudy), then complete thirty days."'

Praise be to Allah, who has created the sun and moon as vital objects for life on Earth. Perhaps we do not spend enough time thinking about what would happen if the sun and moon did not do their job. If that was the case, life on Earth would cease to exist in a matter of hours. Allah talks about the sun and the moon on many occasions in the Qur'an: *'By the sun and its brightness. And by the moon when it follows it. And by the day when it displays it'* (*al-Shams* 91: 1–4). The sun and moon are instrumental features for the last moments of life on Earth. When Allah causes them to be destroyed, their destruction will be witnessed by the last inhabitants of Earth and they will be filled with nothing but terror. Allah says: *'I swear by the Day of Judgement. And I swear by the reproaching soul. Does man think that We will not assemble his bones? Yes. We are able to reassemble it to the fingertips. But man desires to continue in sin. He asks "When is the Day of Judgement?" So when the vision is dazzled and the moon darkens. And the sun and moon are joined. Man will say on that day "Where is a place to escape?"'* (*al-Qiyāmah* 75: 1–10).

One of the great benefits of the sun and moon is that they provide humans with an instrument to measure time. Human beings are a time-orientated species. Our life depends on planning based on time and without it, we will feel disoriented and troubled. We cannot think of life without measuring time. The sun and moon provide us with this facility.

The Islamic calendar is based on the moon, i.e., the calculations of the month and the year are based on the births of the moon. This means that a month cannot be less than 29 days or more than 30 days. When it is the 29th day of the month, a group of Muslims should try to see if they can see the new moon. If a crescent is spotted, then it means that the new month has begun; if not, then that month is considered to have 30 days and the following day commences a new month.

Trying to establish the month of Ramadan is very important, because Muslims are obliged to fast in it. However, there is no need to obsess with the issue of the starting of the moon, come up with calculations or use modern technology to determine if the month has begun—although some scholars have opted for the use of calculations if they provide consistently accurate results. It is simply enough to wait and see if the crescent is visible to the naked eye. If it can be seen, then the new month has started; if not, then the day after thirty days have been completed is the start of the new month.

This hadith is important for the modern day where there is a lot of confusion and obsession regarding the sighting of the moon. This hadith provides an easy guideline to help Muslims to determine the new month.

14

Fasting One Day for the Sake of Allah

عن أَبِي سَعِيدٍ الْخُدْرِيَّ ﷺ قال سَمِعْتُ رَسُولَ اللَّهِ ﷺ يَقُولُ مَنْ صَامَ يَوْمًا فِي سَبِيلِ اللَّهِ تَبَارَكَ وَتَعَالَى بَاعَدَ اللَّهُ وَجْهَهُ عَنِ النَّارِ سَبْعِينَ خَرِيفًا

Abū Sa'īd al-Khudrī ﷺ said: 'I heard the Messenger of Allah ﷺ say: "Whoever fasts one day in the cause of Allah, Allah will separate his face from the Fire by (a distance of) seventy autumns (years)."'

The best relationship a person can have with Allah is not based on a set of mechanical do's and don'ts, but one based on love. A person whose mindset is driven by their love of Allah will find that their worship of Allah is out of love for Him, and such a worshiper will make the best attempt to please Allah. On the other hand, a person who worships Allah because they fear Him, will find that their worship of Allah is also out of fear of Him. Both worshippers are close to Allah and both have merit and favour with their Lord, but a person who worships Allah purely out of love for Him and not only for the fear of His punishment is better. In most cases, a person who worships Allah because they fear Allah's punishment will do the minimum required, but a person who loves Allah and worships Allah out of love for Him will always do more. It is important to note that fear is an important tool within the concept of worship. However, we must make sure to keep love at the forefront. This is just as Ibn al-Qayyim said: 'On his way to Allah, a (believer's) heart is likened to a bird: love is its head, fear and hope are its wings. Hence, when the head and wings are sound, the bird will fly perfectly; if the head is cut, the bird will die and when it loses its wings, it will inevitably become objected to hunting.'[2]

Allah has prescribed certain duties for people to perform and He will hold them to account for that. If they fail to observe these duties, then Allah may choose to punish them. The Prophet Muhammad ﷺ has encouraged us to perform many voluntary acts of worship which come with many great benefits. One such benefit is that it will help a person to make up for the shortfalls or shortcomings in the compulsory acts of worship. The other great benefit of performing voluntary acts of worship is that it gets a person closer to Allah so much so that they become beloved to Allah.

Any act of worship other than the prescribed duties is voluntary worship. In this hadith, the Prophet ﷺ tells us of a promise Allah has made, wherein a person who fasts one day for no purpose other than to seek the pleasure of Allah will be prohibited from the fire of Hell by a distance of seventy autumns. This does not necessarily mean an exact unit of time, rather it is an expression that could mean that Allah will spare the person from the Hellfire.

This hadith teaches us the virtues of fasting purely for the sake of Allah, for His love and seeking His pleasure. There is no act of worshipping Allah better than the one done with sincerity and love.

---

2 Ibn al-Qayyim, *Madarij as-Salikin*, vol. 1, p. 517

The Best Fast

عَنْ عَبْدِ اللَّهِ بْنِ عَمْرٍو قَالَ قَالَ رَسُولُ اللَّهِ ﷺ أَفْضَلُ الصِّيَامِ
صِيَامُ دَاوُدَ عَلَيْهِ السَّلَامُ كَانَ يَصُومُ يَوْمًا وَيُفْطِرُ يَوْمًا

It was narrated that 'Abdullāh ibn 'Amr ؓ said: 'The
Messenger of Allah ﷺ said: "The best of fasting is the fast
of Dāwūd ؑ. He used to fast for one day and break his
fast for one day."'

This hadith points out the most optimal example of voluntary
fasting. In response to 'Abdullāh ibn 'Amr ؓ telling the Prophet
ﷺ that he would like to fast the entire year, the Prophet ﷺ told him
not to, and instead advised him to observe the fast of the Prophet
Dāwūd ؑ. He described the fast of Dāwūd ؑ, which was to fast
every alternate day, to be the best type of voluntary fast.

The eagerness of the Prophet's Companions to perform voluntary
acts of worship is overwhelmingly obvious. They have a special status

with Allah because of the sacrifice they made. This sacrifice was not only with life and money, but their outlook in life as well. They had the love of Allah in their hearts and nothing meant more to them than Allah and His Messenger ﷺ.

The Prophet's Companions pursued a life of emulating the Prophet ﷺ, and some in their eagerness of wanting to do good deeds thought they could surpass him. They were wrong. It is recorded that the Prophet ﷺ once heard three men boasting about their spiritual attainment in pursuing good deeds and doing voluntary acts of worship.[3] One of them boasted that he did not marry as that was a distraction, and he thought celibacy was a virtue because he was able to control the base instinct which Allah created in all human beings. The other boasted he prays the night prayer (*tahajjud*) every night without fail, and the third person boasted that he fasts without a break every day.

The Prophet ﷺ taught his Companions that this was incorrect and that true guidance is in having a balanced life, and that is the Sunnah way of life. The Prophet ﷺ told off these people because they thought that what they were doing was better than what the Prophet ﷺ was doing.

Some Companions loved the Prophet ﷺ so much so that even after his death they would do things the Prophet ﷺ did although they had no religious value, yet they did them only because the Prophet ﷺ did them. For example, it is related that Ibn Umar ؓ was travelling with his friends one day and he came across a point when he was on his camel and he ducked down as if to avoid hitting something. His friends found that to be strange because there were no obstacles to cause Ibn Umar ؓ to duck, so they asked him to explain his action. He told them that he was with the Prophet Muhammad ﷺ and he came to this point and there was a branch sticking out and

3 For reference, please see Hadith 18

so the Prophet ﷺ ducked to avoid it.[4] Ibn Umar ؓ did it because it reminded him of the Prophet ﷺ. Such was the love and eagerness of the Companions to follow the Prophetic way; such was their love of the Prophet Muhammad ﷺ.

Although people have the freedom to worship Allah every night if they choose to do so, it is discouraged. Being balanced is very important and giving the body respite from arduous acts of worship is important for many reasons.

The Prophet's advice about performing voluntary worship in a balanced manner is golden advice for people. He told us that we will get tired of worshipping Allah before Allah gets tired of giving us reward. In other words, be balanced, do not over-exert, and do things consistently even if it is in small amounts.

4 Ahmad, *Musnad*, Hadith no. 4870

16

Six Most Wretched People

عَنْ سَالِمِ بْنِ عَبْدِ اللَّهِ عَنْ أَبِيهِ قَالَ قَالَ رَسُولُ اللَّهِ ﷺ ثَلاَثَةٌ لاَ يَنْظُرُ اللَّهُ عَزَّ وَجَلَّ إِلَيْهِمْ يَوْمَ الْقِيَامَةِ الْعَاقُّ لِوَالِدَيْهِ وَالْمَرْأَةُ الْمُتَرَجِّلَةُ وَالدَّيُّوثُ وَثَلاَثَةٌ لاَ يَدْخُلُونَ الْجَنَّةَ الْعَاقُّ لِوَالِدَيْهِ وَالْمُدْمِنُ عَلَى الْخَمْرِ وَالْمَنَّانُ بِمَا أَعْطَى

Sālim ibn 'Abdullāh narrates from his father that the Messenger of Allah ﷺ said: 'There are three people whom Allah will not look at on the Day of Judgement: The one who disobeys his parents, the woman who imitates men, and the cuckold. And there are three people who will not be allowed to enter Paradise: The one who disobeys his parents, the drunkard, and the one who reminds people of what he has given them.'

Everyone reading this has come across some of those people mentioned in the hadith, if not all of them. It is sad to see such people living their lives without making an effort to change. This hadith serves as an instruction to individuals to reflect and attempt to become better. Self-refection is as important for personal development as prayer is for spirituality. Without self-reflection, a person fails to identify their faults, rectify them and improve themselves. Such a person soon falls into the delusion that they are always right and others are wrong. Their bad actions become the norm for them and their self-proclaimed grandeur becomes their badge of honour. This is why we have to constantly check if we have any of the traits mentioned in this hadith.

This is a very powerful hadith because it describes disgraceful characteristics that many people have. This hadith mentions two groups of people. Both groups are in serious trouble but one group is worse off than the other. The first group the Prophet Muhammad ﷺ tells us of consists of people whom Allah will not look at with mercy, compassion and love. This group consists of three people: The one who disobeys their parents, the woman who imitates men in her outward appearance, and the cuckold who lacks honour in relation to his wife.

The teachings of the Prophet Muhammad ﷺ are clear about a person who is disobedient to their parents, hurts their feelings and is disrespectful to them. Such a person will not only face disgrace in the Hereafter but their end in this life will also be dreadful[5] if they haven't repented and rectified their actions. Being hurtful towards parents appears at the top of the list which signifies the great offence of this

5 This is because they will die as sinners who have committed a major sin. It may be that for such people their destination is a visit from angels who will tear their souls out at the time of their death as Allah says in the Qur'an. (See: Qur'an 79:1)

action. Nothing is gained from behaving poorly towards parents and mistreating them. Hurting them will not bring a person prosperity or good but only misery in this life and the next.

'A woman who wants to act like a man' is an interesting phrase. It does not only mean dressing up like men, but also behaving like them in terms of imitating the blameworthy traits of men such as being loud, boisterous and rumbustious or adopting certain behaviours particular to men in that culture. This hadith is encouraging women to be proud of who they are, to recognize the worth of their own identity and differences from men, rather than feeling as if they have to imitate men. There is a dignified lady-like behaviour women are instructed to observe. It is an expectation in the natural world that creatures will behave in their natural way. Adults are expected to behave as adults and not children, lions are expected to behave like lions and not sheep, water is expected to be water and not fire. When things start to behave in a way other than its natural way, this becomes a cause for concern and creates imbalance in the natural order of life. Self-respect and honour are important in Islam, and men or women who lack this, lack dignity.

A cuckold is a person who lacks dignity, because he does not feel any protective jealousy towards his wife. Perhaps he even finds no problem in his wife acting loosely or inappropriately with other men. Such a person is lacking manhood and the self-respect that Islam has emphasised men to uphold to a high standard.

The second group of people mentioned in the hadith are in greater trouble, because these people will not enter Paradise and are doomed to spend a long time in the fire of Hell. Again, at the top of the list is the person who is disobedient to their parents. This is enough to make us understand how severe this sin is in the Sight of Allah. So, not only will Allah ignore the one who is disobedient to their parents on the Day of Judgement, but will then also cast them into the Hellfire for that sin.

An alcoholic will also find themself in trouble. This refers to a person who has made no effort to stop drinking, repent to Allah and rectify themselves; and instead are disobedient to Allah and become a nuisance to their family and society.

Al-Mannān is a person who reminds people of what they have given them or done for them. When a person does good, but then reminds people that they did something good for them, they lose their reward. Such a person will enter Hell, because what they said and did was hurtful. This is because it is usually the poor and needy that will need help. The actions and favours of a *mannān* were not based on sincerity, but done for ulterior motives. Once good has been done, a person should refrain from talking about it again. Leave it and hope for the best from Allah. If you have done something good for a person, but later that person has hurt you, do not spoil your good deeds by reminding them of what you have done for them. Remember, your reward awaits you with Allah. So leave it to Allah to judge the other person.

May Allah protect us from these evils, and guide us to identify and then rectify our wrongs. May He forgive all of our sins in the Hereafter, and grant us the highest level of Paradise. *Āmīn*.

The Virtues of al-Hajj al-Mabrūr

عَنْ أَبِي هُرَيْرَةَ قَالَ قَالَ رَسُولُ اللَّهِ ﷺ الْحَجَّةُ الْمَبْرُورَةُ لَيْسَ لَهَا جَزَاءٌ إِلاَّ الْجَنَّةُ وَالْعُمْرَةُ إِلَى الْعُمْرَةِ كَفَّارَةٌ لِمَا بَيْنَهُمَا

It was narrated that Abū Hurayrah ؓ said: 'The Messenger of Allah ﷺ said: "*Al-Hajj al-Mabrūr* brings no reward other than Paradise, and from one *'umrah* to another is expiation for what came in between."'

One of the greatest acts of worship is hajj or pilgrimage to Makkah to visit the Holy Mosque known as the Kaaba. In essence, the hajj is a re-enactment of what the great Prophet Ibrāhīm ؑ and his wife did. Prophet Ibrāhīm's actions portrayed the ultimate sacrifice any man can make. He took his wife and new-born child to a hostile and abandoned place and left them there because Allah told him to do so. He was willing to sacrifice his son without hesitation because Allah told him to do so. These tremendous acts of sacrifice were done because Prophet Ibrāhīm ؑ loved Allah. His love for Him made him willing to sacrifice everything for His sake. It is this message of love and sacrifice which Allah wants us to learn. Allah does not want us to sacrifice our sons or leave our families in an abandoned place, but He wants us to understand that sacrifice and love are what made Ibrāhīm ﷺ so special to Allah and what earned him the title 'friend of Allah'.

Allah commands all Muslims who are able, physically and financially, to make a once-in-a-lifetime journey to perform hajj. In this hadith, the Prophet Muhammad ﷺ promised Muslims that the reward for *al-hajj al-mabrūr* is nothing but Paradise. The term *al-hajj al-mabrūr* is very difficult to translate. It requires explanation and does not have an exact translation. The reason for this is because different ahadith have mentioned different components of *al-hajj al-mabrūr*. Once, the Prophet's wife 'Ā'ishah ﷺ said to the Prophet ﷺ: 'O Messenger of Allah, us women consider warfare to be the best of actions. Should we not engage in battle?' He replied: 'No (because war is not suitable for women). Rather, the best form of war (for women) is *hajj al-mabrūr*.'[6]

In another hadith, though a weak one, it is said that *al-hajj al-mabrūr* is: 'Giving food and spreading peace' while Ibn 'Abbās said it is: '*'Ajj* and *thajj*,' meaning raising one's voice saying '*labbayk*' and slaughtering the sacrificial animals in order to feed the pilgrims.[7]

Some scholars maintain that *al-hajj al-mabrūr* is when a pilgrim does not weaken their hajj by committing any sins. Others say that it is an accepted hajj or one in which there is no ostentation or reputation-seeking, or one in which the person performing it observes all the rites of hajj in its complete and proper way.

All these explanations shed light on the meaning of *al-hajj al-mabrūr,* through which we can observe three main components to *al-hajj al-mabrūr.*

---

6 Al-Bukhari, *Sahih al-Bukhari*, Hadith no. 2784

7 Ibn Majah, *Sunan Ibn Majah*, Hadith no. 2924

Sincerity

Sincerity is needed in order for your hajj to be *mabrūr* (accepted). Your intention must be that you seek Allah's pleasure alone in performing it. There must be no ostentation, showing-off or reputation-seeking in it. You can elevate your intention by intending sincere repentance such that your spiritual state becomes higher after hajj. After hajj, you should no longer be neglectful of your obligations nor persistently commit minor sins or any major sins.

Lawful (*Ḥalāl*) Provisions

The pilgrim should not fund their hajj with money that is unlawful or *ḥarām*. This includes money spent on food, clothing, transport and other expenses incurred during the hajj as well as the maintenance of dependents left behind such as the wife and children. Money gained through unlawful means will not make an acceptable hajj, although the obligation of hajj is fulfilled. The money should not be from unlawful means such as theft, bribery, fraud, usury, cheating, selling drugs and alcohol and the like.

Excellence in Worship

During hajj a person should perform the rituals of hajj according to Islam and protect the heart and limbs from committing sin. They should busy themselves with remembering Allah and not fall into argumentation or foul speech. The bare minimum in order for the hajj to be *mabrūr* is to perform the obligatory parts of the hajj as well as to refrain from the things that invalidate it and the things that are prohibited during it.

18

False Piety

عَنْ أَنَسٍ أَنَّ نَفَرًا مِنْ أَصْحَابِ النَّبِيِّ ﷺ قَالَ بَعْضُهُمْ لاَ أَتَزَوَّجُ النِّسَاءَ وَقَالَ بَعْضُهُمْ لاَ آكُلُ اللَّحْمَ وَقَالَ بَعْضُهُمْ لاَ أَنَامُ عَلَى فِرَاشٍ وَقَالَ بَعْضُهُمْ أَصُومُ فَلاَ أُفْطِرُ فَبَلَغَ ذَلِكَ رَسُولَ اللَّهِ ﷺ فَحَمِدَ اللَّهَ وَأَثْنَى عَلَيْهِ ثُمَّ قَالَ مَا بَالُ أَقْوَامٍ يَقُولُونَ كَذَا وَكَذَا لَكِنِّي أُصَلِّي وَأَنَامُ وَأَصُومُ وَأُفْطِرُ وَأَتَزَوَّجُ النِّسَاءَ فَمَنْ رَغِبَ عَنْ سُنَّتِي فَلَيْسَ مِنِّي

It was narrated from Anas ؓ that there was a group of the Companions of the Prophet ﷺ, one of whom said: 'I will not marry women,' another said: 'I will not eat meat,' another said: 'I will not sleep on a bed,' and another said: 'I will constantly fast and not break my fast.' News of that reached the Messenger of Allah ﷺ so he praised Allah then said: 'What is the matter with people who say such and such? I pray and I sleep, I fast and I break my fast, and I marry women. Whoever turns away from my Sunnah is not of me.'

Allah has created humanity to worship Him, but He did not leave it at that. He created us and then sent us teachers to show us how to worship Allah. It does not matter how intelligent a person may think they are, it is not possible for them to understand how to worship Allah in the correct way without a teacher. It is for this reason that Allah has sent prophets to humankind to show them the right way. Allah commands people to follow their Prophets and Allah commands Muslims of this ummah to follow the Prophet Muhammad ﷺ. Following him is guidance and disobeying him is misguidance.

There are two very important messages this hadith teaches Muslims. The first is the importance of following the Sunnah of the Prophet Muhammad ﷺ. Allah has created humankind and fashioned us with wants and desires. Not all the desires humans have are wrong and need to be suppressed. For example, the need to eat is a natural part of being human. We desire to eat well and have delicious food. This is something most humans desire. There is nothing wrong in pursuing this need, but what is wrong is pursuing unlawful means to gain food or eating unlawful products which Allah and His Messenger ﷺ have prohibited. In like manner, the need to get married is a natural need and there is nothing wrong in pursuing it. There is a misconception that trying to suppress these natural human desires is an act of piety, and that the stronger the desire is, the more rewardable its suppression is. This is false.

When the Prophet ﷺ heard of some people boasting about their assumption of what piety is, he wanted to teach them the correct way and warn them of ignoring this advice. He told them in clear terms that his way of life is the way that Allah has endorsed and closeness to Allah can only be achieved in that way; and ignoring this advice means that those people can never attain the true piety that they seek. This shows us the importance of following the Sunnah and that closeness to Allah can only be gained through the Sunnah.

The second message this hadith teaches us is the warning of being extreme in religion. There is no reward, no goodness, no blessings in being extreme in worshipping Allah. Avoiding the lawful, especially if it was done and encouraged by the Prophet ﷺ is pointless. Islam instructs having a balanced life. Going to extremes in trying to be religious is harmful for our mental health and spiritual development. Extremism and not following the Sunnah only give a false sense of piety. Ultimately, it goes against Islam and it does not lead to closeness to Allah.

19

Wedding Celebrations

عَنْ مُحَمَّدِ بْنِ حَاطِبٍ قَالَ قَالَ رَسُولُ اللَّهِ ﷺ فَصْلُ مَا بَيْنَ الْحَلَالِ وَالْحَرَامِ الدُّفُّ وَالصَّوْتُ فِي النِّكَاحِ

It was narrated that Muḥammad ibn Ḥāṭib ﷺ said: 'The Messenger of Allah ﷺ said: "What differentiates between the lawful and the unlawful is the *duff* and the voice (singing) for the wedding."'

One of the greatest moments in anyone's life is when they are getting married. It signals a landmark of reaching a certain age, and it tells the world that a person has become responsible, mature and prudent. Marriage is a sacred institution observed by all cultures and civilisations. It is sacred because it is a promise between two people to look after each other, care for one another, raise a family together and be productive in society. Allah has created humankind and given us certain needs and desires. Marriage is sacred because it is the lawful avenue for people to address their basic needs. It is the bond of partnership in which people lawfully raise a family. It provides security and safety for children and it is the best environment for children to be raised in.

The marriage ceremony is a joyous occasion, a time for celebrations and parties. It is a time for jokes, merriment, dressing up, eating and drinking. This is universal and every culture agrees to it. Every culture has their own unique traditions for weddings, pre-wedding celebrations and after wedding celebrations. Everyone, young, old, male and female, collectively participate in making the wedding fun and enjoyable.

There are two things this hadith teaches Muslims. Firstly, Islam requires a wedding to be made public and that it must have some sort of announcement. Secondly, fun and celebratory activities are allowed. Getting married in secrecy is seriously questionable. A wedding feast, known in Arabic as *walīmah*, goes some way in telling people that a person has married. Islam regards a wedding as a very joyous occasion and as such it has made many dispensations to help create an atmosphere of celebration. Islam has allowed beating the *duff* during weddings to announce to society that a wedding has taken place. Not everyone in society may have the ability to hold a *walīmah* or invite everyone, but everyone can hear the sound of the *duff*. The only musical instrument that is permissible is the *duff*, and not others such as the *tabl* or the drums. The difference between them is that the *tabl* is covered on both sides whereas the daff is open on one side and covered on the other. Islam has allowed singing permissible songs in celebration, gender-segregated dancing, and other types of celebratory activities too.

It must be noted that although some Islamic rules are relaxed for wedding celebrations, all unlawful acts must be clearly avoided such as free-mixing between men and women and wearing inappropriate clothes.

20

Forced Marriage in Islam

عَنْ عَائِشَةَ أَنَّ فَتَاةً دَخَلَتْ عَلَيْهَا فَقَالَتْ إِنَّ أَبِي زَوَّجَنِي ابْنَ أَخِيهِ لِيَرْفَعَ بِي خَسِيسَتَهُ وَأَنَا كَارِهَةٌ قَالَتِ اجْلِسِي حَتَّى يَأْتِيَ النَّبِيُّ ﷺ فَجَاءَ رَسُولُ اللَّهِ ﷺ فَأَخْبَرَتْهُ فَأَرْسَلَ إِلَى أَبِيهَا فَدَعَاهُ فَجَعَلَ الأَمْرَ إِلَيْهَا فَقَالَتْ يَا رَسُولَ اللَّهِ قَدْ أَجَزْتُ مَا صَنَعَ أَبِي وَلَكِنْ أَرَدْتُ أَنْ أَعْلَمَ أَلِلنِّسَاءِ مِنَ الأَمْرِ شَيْءٌ

It was narrated from 'Ā'ishah ﵂ that a girl came to her and said: 'My father married me to his brother's son so that he might raise his own status thereby, and I was unwilling.' She said: 'Sit here until the Prophet ﷺ comes.' Then the Messenger of Allah ﷺ came, and I told him (what she had said). He sent word to her father, calling him, and he left it to her to decide. She said: 'O Messenger of Allah, I accept what my father did, but I wanted to know whether women have any say in the matter.'

Allah has created everything, and He has granted everything its rights. No one has the right to violate these rights and if they do, they will be accountable for it on the Day of Judgement. Children have rights over their parents and their parents have rights over them. Teachers have rights over their students, and they have rights over their teachers. The animals have rights, the environment has rights and Allah has His rights.

The rights humans have are comprehensive and every member of the human species, regardless of age and status, have their own rights. These rights come into existence as early as when a child is a foetus. These rights are known as *ḥuqūq al-'ibād*.

This hadith is talking about the right of a girl to marry the person of her choice. Just as children will be held accountable if they mistreat their parents, so will parents be answerable if they mistreat their children.

Many ahadith speak about being dutiful to parents, but parents must know that their children have rights too. They cannot infringe on these rights. One such right God has given to all humans is their right to choose whom they want to marry.

Unfortunately, there are some parents who ignore this right and seek to interfere wrongly in the future of their children. Mostly, girls end up being at the receiving end of being forced to marry without their consent or consultation. This has nothing to do with Islam, and in fact it goes against the rulings in Islam. This hadith is a clear testimony that Islam rejects forced marriage or marrying children without their consent and consultation.

Once, during the time of the Prophet ﷺ a man married his

daughter to his nephew for personal gain without consulting his daughter. She was upset about this and so she came to the Prophet Muhammad ﷺ to complain about her father. When the Prophet ﷺ heard what her father did, he summoned her father to hear his side of the story. The story matched, and the Prophet ﷺ told the girl that she can break the marriage if she wanted to or continue it; it was her choice. The girl said she was actually happy to accept the marriage, but just wanted to know if Islam gave women the right to decide.

There can be nothing more selfish than for parents to deny their children the chance to pursue happiness in life. It is their duty to help and support their children and teach them what is lawful and what is unlawful. Marriage in particular is something that affects our lives significantly, and should not be treated as a means to return a favour or climb the social ladder. Islam has given people the choice to marry people of their choosing. This is the right Allah and His Messenger ﷺ gave us and it must be upheld unapologetically.

21

The Mourning Period

قَالَتْ زَيْنَبُ بنت أبى سلمة دَخَلْتُ عَلَى زَيْنَبَ بِنْتِ جَحْشٍ حِينَ تُوُفِّيَ أَخُوهَا وَقَدْ دَعَتْ بِطِيبٍ وَمَسَّتْ مِنْهُ ثُمَّ قَالَتْ وَاللَّهِ مَا لِي بِالطِّيبِ مِنْ حَاجَةٍ غَيْرَ أَنِّي سَمِعْتُ رَسُولَ اللَّهِ ﷺ يَقُولُ عَلَى الْمِنْبَرِ لاَ يَحِلُّ لاِمْرَأَةٍ تُؤْمِنُ بِاللَّهِ وَالْيَوْمِ الآخِرِ تَحِدُّ عَلَى مَيِّتٍ فَوْقَ ثَلاَثِ لَيَالٍ إِلاَّ عَلَى زَوْجٍ أَرْبَعَةَ أَشْهُرٍ وَعَشْرًا

Zaynab bint Abī Salamah ﵂ said: 'I visited Zaynab bint Jaḥsh ﵂ when her brother died, and she called for some perfume and put some on. Then she said: "By Allah, I do not have any need for perfume but I heard the Messenger of Allah ﷺ say on the *minbar* (pulpit): 'It is not permissible for any woman who believes in Allah and the Last Day to mourn for anyone who dies for more than three days, except for a husband, four months and ten days.'"'

Islam came to correct many unfair customs that were prevalent amongst the Arabs at the time. It did not necessarily abolish all of these customs, but it did keep them within the boundaries of balance and sound creed. From the customs which Islam kept within appropriate boundaries is mourning (*ḥidād*) when a relative passes away. This involved abstaining from washing, perfume, beautification, and leaving the home, as a symbol of sadness for the deceased.

Islam accepted this custom of mourning because sadness is a natural feeling and to show sadness to others can be a sign of respect to the relatives of the deceased. However, this period was limited by Islam to only three days. Hence, a woman is allowed to abstain from the above for no more than three days. This is to avoid any extremism with regards to the deceased of the sort that existed before Islam. This does not mean that crying or sadness are not allowed because these are natural internal feelings that are sometimes beyond control. However, our outward reaction must be one of balance and being pleased with the decree of Allah. Zaynab bint Jaḥsh ﵂, the wife of the Prophet Muhammad ﷺ, intentionally used perfume a few days after the passing of her brother to teach those around her that symbols of mourning are not allowed beyond three days, except in the case of the death of a husband.

When a woman's husband dies, she goes through an obligatory waiting period (*'iddah*) of four months and ten days, as established by the Qur'an. In this period, she should avoid perfume or beautification, and she is unable to marry until this period is complete. However, unlike pre-Islamic customs, she should still keep herself clean and she can leave her house when there is a need during this period. The mourning period for the husband is longer because of the strong marital bond that exists between the spouses. The wisdoms behind the *'iddah* are many, including being a sign of respect for the husband, his family, for the wife to take her time to recover, and to ensure that she is not pregnant with the child of the deceased. At the same time, it is a waiting period which is not burdensome for a woman to wait before she remarries.

22

Obedience to the Leader is a Must

عَنِ ابْنِ عُمَرَ قَالَ قَالَ رَسُولُ اللَّهِ ﷺ عَلَى الْمَرْءِ الْمُسْلِمِ السَّمْعُ وَالطَّاعَةُ فِيمَا أَحَبَّ وَكَرِهَ إِلاَّ أَنْ يُؤْمَرَ بِمَعْصِيَةٍ فَإِذَا أُمِرَ بِمَعْصِيَةٍ فَلاَ سَمْعَ وَلاَ طَاعَةَ

It was narrated that Ibn Umar ؓ said: 'The Messenger of Allah ﷺ said: "The Muslim must hear and obey whether he likes it or not, unless he is commanded to commit an act of disobedience. If he is commanded to commit an act of disobedience, then he is not required to hear and obey."'

There is no doubt that ultimate obedience should only be to Allah. It is only Allah Almighty who speaks the perfect truth. Anything that comes from anyone besides Allah has the potential of being flawed, due to the imperfect nature of created beings. Allah says about the Qur'an: *'Had it been from anyone besides Allah, they would surely have found in it many discrepancies' (al-Nisā'* 4: 82). However,

Allah sent Prophets to guide people to the path of truth and guidance. Allah therefore obliged all people to obey their Prophets. Since Allah aided His Prophets and guided them, obeying the Prophets is equal to obeying Allah. Both the Qur'an and Sunnah have taught Muslims and commanded them to obey some other categories of people, besides Allah and His Prophets. For instance, the Qur'an commands us to obey scholars and rulers. *'Obey Allah, His Messenger, and those in authority among you. Should you disagree on anything, then refer it to Allah and His Messenger, if you [truly] believe in Allah and the Last Day'* (*al-Nisā'* 4: 59). Those in authority are the scholars and rulers. Similarly, Islam teaches us the importance of obeying parents and husbands, too. However, there is a vital difference between obeying Allah and His Messenger on one hand and obeying other humans on the other.

Obedience to the former is because they are our source of guidance. The Qur'an and Prophetic teachings are the only true sources of guidance which all Muslims are bound to follow. Obedience to the latter, however, is not because they are divinely guided in all their words and actions. In fact, they may at times be misguided and ignorant. However, Islam encourages obedience to them for the greater good that stems from doing so. This does not mean that parents, husbands or anyone in authority is at liberty to abuse their position by being unjust, unfair, abusive or oppressive. You should know that if you do wrong to anyone, you will be sinful and accountable in front of Allah on the Day of Judgement.

Obedience to rulers and scholars ensures societal stability and order. It helps to minimise division and disorder. It ensures that Muslims can worship Allah safely and comfortably. It means that Muslims are a strong unit prepared to protect themselves and call to Allah. However, because the obedience of rulers is secondary to the obedience of Allah, they are not to be obeyed if this leads to disobeying Allah. Other than that, one should be patient and keep within the commands of the leadership for the greater good of society. Being patient with a corrupt ruler is often better than going against him, thus causing unrest, disorder, and bloodshed.

Bad Rulers

عَنْ كَعْبِ بْنِ عُجْرَةَ قَالَ خَرَجَ عَلَيْنَا رَسُولُ اللَّهِ ﷺ وَنَحْنُ تِسْعَةٌ فَقَالَ إِنَّهُ سَتَكُونُ بَعْدِى أُمَرَاءُ مَنْ صَدَّقَهُمْ بِكَذِبِهِمْ وَأَعَانَهُمْ عَلَى ظُلْمِهِمْ فَلَيْسَ مِنِّي وَلَسْتُ مِنْهُ وَلَيْسَ بِوَارِدٍ عَلَيَّ الْحَوْضَ وَمَنْ لَمْ يُصَدِّقْهُمْ بِكَذِبِهِمْ وَلَمْ يُعِنْهُمْ عَلَى ظُلْمِهِمْ فَهُوَ مِنِّي وَأَنَا مِنْهُ وَهُوَ وَارِدٌ عَلَيَّ الْحَوْضَ

It was narrated that Ka'b ibn 'Ujrah ﵁ said: 'The Messenger of Allah ﷺ came out to us, and there were nine of us. He said: "After me there will be rulers; whoever believes in their lies and helps them in their wrongdoing is not of me, and I am not of him, and he will not come to me at the Fountain (*ḥawḍ*). Whoever does not believe their lies and does not help them in their wrongdoing, he is of me, and I am of him, and he will come to me at the Fountain.'"

It is an unfortunate fact that from time to time, people are blighted with oppressive rulers who believe that people should serve them and make sure that they live, eat and stay in safety. The comfortable life leadership gives, is too good to give up and power and authority become too addictive to lose. Being a bad leader means that the person knows people do not like him and want him out, but in order to stay in power, the leader oppresses people and scares them. The previous hadith spoke about the importance of obedience to the leaders for the sake of unity, order and protection. However, this hadith clarifies that this does not necessitate supporting oppression and injustice.

The Prophet Muhammad ﷺ explicitly prohibited obeying rulers if they command one to commit a sin. If a ruler ordered a person to kill someone who is innocent, it would not be permissible to obey him. Likewise, it is prohibited to aid rulers in any type of oppression or wrongdoing, such as usurping the property of others unjustly and imprisoning those who are innocent. Rather, those who believe that their advice may be heard should advise rulers to fear Allah and remind them of the great responsibility of taking authority over the people. Scholars who have a position in the state have an additional responsibility to give such advice. This was the way of the righteous scholars of the past from the Prophet's Companions until today.

In this hadith, the Prophet Muhammad ﷺ even prohibited Muslims from believing the lies of rulers. Although we should not make negative assumptions of leaders without clear proof, this hadith indicates that we should not be so naive that we accept everything a ruler says, either. This is because accepting everything a ruler says without careful consideration can have severe consequences. It may lead scholars and other people of influence in society – although perhaps out of good will – to aid their ruler in his injustice. It is not so easy to remain firm upon the truth in the face of state authorities. Most people waver and become weak in such situations. To oppose the lies of those in authority and refuse to support their wrongdoing requires patience and strength. This is why the reward of doing so is so great. The one who keeps firm to the truth despite fearing harm is worthy of the high status mentioned by the Prophet ﷺ in this hadith.

24

Target Practice and Looking after Living Creatures

عَنِ ابْنِ عَبَّاسٍ أَنَّ رَسُولَ اللَّهِ ﷺ قَالَ لاَ تَتَّخِذُوا شَيْئًا فِيهِ الرُّوحُ غَرَضًا

It was narrated that Ibn 'Abbās ﵄ said: 'The Messenger of Allah ﷺ forbade us from using anything with a soul as a target.'

Allah has honoured humankind. He gave us abilities and blessings which raise us above the rank of other beings on Earth. Humans have been favoured mainly because of our intellect. This favouring has made us worthy of being Allah's deputies on Earth, as we are told in the Qur'an. Humans not only have a responsibility to uphold justice on the Earth, but to also look after it and all species on it. Allah, the Creator of Earth's animals, gave humans the freedom to benefit from animals in various ways. *'And He created the cattle for you as a source of warmth, food, and [many other] benefits; and in them there is beauty for you when you bring them home and when you take them out to pasture.*

And they carry your loads to [distant] lands which you could not otherwise reach without great hardship. Surely your Lord is Ever Gracious, Most Merciful' (*al-Naḥl* 16: 5–7). However, with these blessings comes responsibilities. The permission to benefit from animals in these many ways is not a concession to mistreat animals or to cause them pain, physical or psychological. If some harm is necessary, such as in the case of slaughter for food or when they cause a risk to humans, then this must be done in the best and most gentle way possible without prolonging their suffering.

In this hadith, the Prophet Muhammad ﷺ prohibits using animals as a target to shoot arrows at for practice or leisure. This does not include hunting for food. The Qur'an is clear about allowing hunting for food. However, the hadith speaks of making animals a target for pleasure and entertainment, because this involves harming animals for no valid reason, an action that is immoral and strictly prohibited in Islam. Islam prohibits all types of blood sport and killing of animals as a trophy. Unfortunately, we still see these practices of providing entertainment through allowing animals to suffer. Bullfighting is just one of many examples of this. In fact, the Prophet Muhammad ﷺ told us of a woman who will enter Hellfire because of a cat that she caged and did not feed until it starved to death. This act of cruelty earned her a place in Hell. Hence, as much as Allah has honoured humans and allowed us to benefit from animals, He has placed a serious responsibility upon us to treat animals and all living creatures in the most kind and caring manner.

25

Splitting of the Chest

عَنْ أَنَسِ بْنِ مَالِكٍ أَنَّ الصَّلَوَاتِ فُرِضَتْ بِمَكَّةَ وَأَنَّ مَلَكَيْنِ أَتَيَا رَسُولَ اللَّهِ ﷺ فَذَهَبَا بِهِ إِلَى زَمْزَمَ فَشَقَّا بَطْنَهُ وَأَخْرَجَا حَشْوَهُ فِي طَسْتٍ مِنْ ذَهَبٍ فَغَسَلَاهُ بِمَاءِ زَمْزَمَ ثُمَّ كَبَسَا جَوْفَهُ حِكْمَةً وَعِلْمًا

It was narrated from Anas ibn Mālik ﵁ that the prayers were enjoined in Makkah, and that two angels came to the Messenger of Allah ﷺ and took him to Zamzam, where they split open his stomach and took out his innards in a basin of gold, and washed them with Zamzam water, then they filled his heart with wisdom and knowledge.

All the Prophets that Allah sent to be guides for humankind were themselves human beings. They ate, drank, and lived like normal humans. However, they were supported by Divine guidance so that they may deliver the message of Allah in the best and most accurate way. They were guided by Allah not only to have a perfect understanding of Allah's guidance, but also so that they will have pure hearts which were vessels of firm faith and total awareness of Allah. Every human is prone to desires that can lead them to misguided beliefs or actions. Human hearts are delicate vessels that are prone to sin, and also become easily damaged through partaking in sin. For the Prophet Muhammad ﷺ to be a true guide, it would not suffice for him to verbally deliver the message of Allah to humankind. Rather, a true guide can only be one who himself is a role model, living by the guidance that Allah wills for His creation.

This hadith talks about an incident where the Prophet's heart was cleansed by the angels and purified by the sacred water of Zamzam. It cleansed the influence of Satan on the Prophet ﷺ and protected him from the misguidance that all other humans are prone to suffer. In another hadith, it was said to the Prophet ﷺ, after this cleansing took place, 'This is Satan's portion from you [being washed away].' His heart was then filled with wisdom and knowledge. In another hadith, it is stated that the Prophet's heart was also filled with *īmān* (faith). Strong faith, sound knowledge, and wisdom are the three prerequisites for a competent leader and guide. Strong faith to protect oneself from carnal desires, sound knowledge to protect oneself from ignorance, and wisdom to ensure that this knowledge is applied in the best and most appropriate way at any given circumstance. This Divine purification is what makes the Prophetic Sunnah the purest, wisest, and most noble example for those who come after him.

26

Work and Earnings

عَنْ عَائِشَةَ أَنَّ النَّبِيَّ ﷺ قال إِنَّ أَطْيَبَ مَا أَكَلَ الرَّجُلُ مِنْ كَسْبِهِ وَوَلَدُهُ مِنْ كَسْبِهِ

It was narrated from 'Ā'ishah رضي الله عنها that the Prophet ﷺ said: 'The best (most pure) food that a man eats is that which he has earned himself, and his child (his child's wealth) is part of his earning.'

The purest and most honourable thing that one can eat and consume is that which they have earned through the work of their own hands. Many statements of the Prophet Muhammad ﷺ encouraged people to work for their earnings, even if this is done through the simplest of jobs. This hadith informs Muslims that just as there is no harm in eating from what one has earned, there is no blame on them for eating from the earnings of their children. That is because the relationship that exists between parent and child should never be one in which a parent feels as though they require permission from their child the way they do with another person. The status of the parent is greater than that. In addition, it would be a great burden for many people if permission were always needed, since many parents live in the same house or nearby their children, thus often being around one another. The Qur'an gives similar guidance when it comes to eating from the homes of close relatives, such as our brothers, sisters, uncles, aunts, and close friends. This is detailed in verse 61 of *Surah al-Nūr*. This gives people the flexibility that they need and also strengthens the ties of relationship between them.

While we should encourage these teachings amongst people, one should keep in mind various customs and what people normally consider acceptable or unacceptable. This is to avoid disputes or cutting ties of kinship. When it comes to a parent taking from the wealth of the child, this hadith seems to allow that. Many jurists have said that this hadith refers to when a parent is in need, since a child is still the owner of their own wealth and it cannot be used without their permission. However, exception is given to parents to use the wealth of their child if they need to or if it is something not so significant, due to the great status the parents have. In fact, a child is responsible for providing for their parents if they are in need, just as the parents provided for the child when he or she was young. It is imperative for children to know that they are not doing their parents a favour by supporting them financially, rather they are fulfilling an obligation due on themselves.

27

Abundance of Wealth and Trading: Signs of the Day of Judgement

عَنْ عَمْرِو بْنِ تَغْلِبَ قَالَ قَالَ رَسُولُ اللَّهِ ﷺ إِنَّ مِنْ أَشْرَاطِ
السَّاعَةِ أَنْ يَفْشُوَ الْمَالُ وَيَكْثُرَ وَتَفْشُوَ التِّجَارَةُ وَيَظْهَرَ الْعِلْمُ
وَيَبِيعَ الرَّجُلُ الْبَيْعَ فَيَقُولَ لاَ حَتَّى أَسْتَأْمِرَ تَاجِرَ بَنِي فُلاَنٍ
وَيُلْتَمَسَ فِي الْحَيِّ الْعَظِيمِ الْكَاتِبُ فَلاَ يُوجَدُ

'Amr ibn Taghlib ؓ reported that the Messenger of Allah ﷺ said: 'One of the signs of the Hour will be that wealth becomes widespread and abundant, and trade will become widespread, and knowledge [the pen] will appear. A man will try to sell something and will say, "No, not until I consult the merchant of Banū so-and-so," and people will look throughout a vast area for a scribe and will not find one.'

The Qur'an has mentioned some of the signs of the nearing of the Day of Judgment and authentic Hadith literature mentions these signs in more detail. The ahadith speaking of these signs should not be merely treated as the transmission of factual information, rather, we ought to have a reflective attitude towards the words of Allah and His Prophet ﷺ regarding these matters. An action is not blameworthy by the mere virtue of it being counted amongst the signs of the Hour, but their mention should make us spend some time to ponder and contemplate over it. In this hadith, we are told that wealth and trading will become widespread. One of the major concerns of people will be maximising their wealth.

In another hadith, the Prophet Muhammad ﷺ tells us that a time will come when people will not be interested in how they obtain their wealth, whether through legitimate or sinful means. Their only concern will be to maximise wealth regardless of what it takes to do so. This attitude is one of the main reasons why blessing is removed from wealth, such that one may have a high income, but feel as though they are in constant financial difficulty. Being cautious about earning only through pure and permissible means will bring blessing to our wealth, so that a modest income will make us feel as though we are never in a crunch and always financially comfortable.

Regarding the spread of 'knowledge', another wording of the same hadith in the *Musnad* of Aḥmad states instead that the use of the 'pen' will increase. This clarifies the meaning of the spread of 'knowledge' mentioned in the narration here. This means that writing of knowledge and printing books will increase, although this is no more than rewriting information. True knowledge will be lost.

This hadith is remarkable in that we can see it happening in front of our eyes. Never before in the history of the human race has wealth been so abundantly available, so much so that some governments simply print out money to create wealth. Trillions of pounds are traded every day, a figure that was unheard of during the time of the

Prophet Muhammad ﷺ. We are living in an age where we can see widespread trading. Every person can trade on e-Bay or Amazon and sell small to big items. The real question is, how close is the end of this world? And how prepared are we for it?

28

Dyeing the Hair

عَنْ أَبِي هُرَيْرَةَ أَنَّ رَسُولَ اللَّهِ ﷺ قَالَ الْيَهُودُ وَالنَّصَارَى لاَ تَصْبُغُ فَخَالِفُوهُمْ

It was narrated from Abū Hurayrah رضي الله عنه that: 'The Messenger of Allah ﷺ said: "The Jews and Christians do not dye their hair, so be different from them."'

If one's beard has become white, then it is from the Sunnah to dye it. The father of Abu Bakr al-Ṣiddīq رضي الله عنه once came to the Prophet ﷺ who saw that his hair was completely white. The Prophet ﷺ said that he should dye his hair but avoid black.[8] There are varying narrations about whether the Prophet Muhammad ﷺ dyed his hair or not. Anas ibn Mālik رضي الله عنه said that the Prophet ﷺ did not need to dye his hair, because he only had very few white hairs. However, Abu Bakr and

---

8 Muslim, *Sahih Muslim*, Hadith no. 2102

Umar ﷺ both used to dye their beards, as well as other Companions. Some scholars suggested that the Jews and Christians at that time would avoid dyeing their hair because they viewed this to contradict the servitude and humility that they should be upon. However, Islam did not accept this and encouraged dyeing a beard that had become white. The Prophet ﷺ wanted to emphasise to the Muslims that Islam suffices them. Therefore, he would often remind them to not imitate the Jews and Christians around them.

Dyeing a white beard also provides a more youthful appearance which has a positive psychological impact on the person himself and those around him. It is recommended for this to be done using *henna* and *khatam* (a type of plant used for dying hair), though other materials can be used too. This hadith refers specifically to dyeing the hair of the head and beard when they have become completely or mostly white. It does not encourage everyone to dye their hair regardless of their hair colour. Dyeing the hair for people in general is not a Sunnah, but it is permissible, particularly for women who do so for beautification purposes. However, this should be restricted to natural hair colour, such as brown, blonde, and red, so that one keeps a natural appearance.

It is worth noting that there is a slight disagreement regarding dyeing the hair black. Some scholars believed that dyeing the hair black is not permissible while many other scholars believed that it is permissible to do so. Ibn Abī 'Āṣim wrote about this topic and he chose to follow the opinion that it is permissible to dye the hair black. He responded to the hadith narrated by Ibn 'Abbās ﷺ in which he said, 'By the end of time there will be people who dye their hair black, they will not even smell the fragrance of Paradise,'[9] by saying that the hadith does not include evidence on the undesirability of dyeing hair black; rather, it describes one trait of certain people who will live

9 Nasa'i, *Sunan al-Nasa'i*, Hadith no. 5075

during the end of time. However, it is more appropriate for men to refrain from using black dye and avoid the scholarly disagreement over dyeing hair black, altogether.

29

There is no Harm in a Woman Asking a Man to Marry Her

عَنْ سَهْلِ بْنِ سَعْدٍ أَنَّ رَسُولَ اللَّهِ ﷺ جَاءَتْهُ امْرَأَةٌ فَقَالَتْ يَا رَسُولَ
اللَّهِ إِنِّي قَدْ وَهَبْتُ نَفْسِي لَكَ فَقَامَتْ قِيَامًا طَوِيلاً فَقَامَ رَجُلٌ
فَقَالَ زَوِّجْنِيهَا إِنْ لَمْ يَكُنْ لَكَ بِهَا حَاجَةٌ قَالَ رَسُولُ اللَّهِ ﷺ
هَلْ عِنْدَكَ شَيْءٌ؟ قَالَ مَا أَجِدُ شَيْئًا قَالَ الْتَمِسْ وَلَوْ خَاتَمًا مِنْ
حَدِيدٍ فَالْتَمَسَ فَلَمْ يَجِدْ شَيْئًا فَقَالَ لَهُ رَسُولُ اللَّهِ ﷺ هَلْ مَعَكَ
مِنَ الْقُرْآنِ شَيْءٌ؟ قَالَ نَعَمْ سُورَةُ كَذَا وَسُورَةُ كَذَا لِسُوَرٍ سَمَّاهَا
قَالَ رَسُولُ اللَّهِ ﷺ قَدْ زَوَّجْتُكَهَا عَلَى مَا مَعَكَ مِنَ الْقُرْآنِ

It was narrated from Sahl ibn Sa‘d رضي الله عنه that a woman came to the Messenger of Allah ﷺ and said: ‘O Messenger of Allah, I give myself in marriage to you.’ She stood for some time, then a man stood up and said: ‘Marry her to me if you do not want to marry her.’ The Messenger of

Allah ﷺ said: 'Do you have anything (as dowry)?' He said: 'I cannot find anything.' The Messenger of Allah ﷺ said: 'Look (for something), even if it is only an iron ring.' He looked but he could not find anything. The Messenger of Allah ﷺ said to him: 'Have you (memorised) anything of the Qur'an?' He said: 'Yes, such and such chapters, naming them.' The Messenger of Allah ﷺ said: 'I marry her to you for what you know of the Qur'an.'

The Prophet's actions are to be followed by every Muslim because he is the living role model that Allah placed on Earth. However, the Companions of the Prophet ﷺ and the scholars of Islam are in agreement that some rulings were specific to the Prophet ﷺ alone and did not apply to any other Muslim. There are many reasons for this, including Allah wanting to honour his Prophet due to his already lofty status, the role of prophethood possibly requiring some things which were specific to him, and the Prophet ﷺ having a position of respect and obedience amongst the Muslims not enjoyed by anyone else. From these specific rulings to him are that a woman could give herself to the Prophet ﷺ in marriage even without a *mahr* (dowry). Such a marriage is not valid for any other Muslim, as the Qur'an explicitly states: '... *and a believing woman who offers herself to the Prophet [without dowry] if he is interested in marrying her; [this being] exclusively for you, not for the rest of the believers'* (*al-Aḥzāb* 33: 50).

Muslim scholars, including Imam al-Bukhārī and Imam al-Nasā'ī, stated that this hadith indicates that a woman is allowed to propose herself in marriage to a righteous man. If he agrees, they then proceed with the marriage contract with all its necessary conditions. This may be seen as inappropriate in some cultures, but there is nothing in

Islam which prevents it. The male guardian of a woman can suggest his daughter or sister or other relative to a man for marriage. Similarly, a woman can make this proposal herself or by sending someone to do this on her behalf. In fact, far from being inappropriate, if done to the right person and in a respectful manner, it shows the concern of this woman to marry someone righteous. Additionally, many women may not have Muslim relatives who can help her to marry a suitable husband, so she may find herself in a position to propose herself if a suitable man came by.

This hadith also teaches Muslims that marriage should be made easy for people rather than be made into a burdensome cultural practice which hinders many from getting married. It also teaches Muslims that it is obligatory for men to give the woman he marries a dowry. Finally, the hadith also teaches that the dowry should not be extravagant.

30

The Seven People who will be Under the Shade of Allah's Throne

عَنْ أَبِي هُرَيْرَةَ أَنَّ رَسُولَ اللَّهِ ﷺ قَالَ سَبْعَةٌ يُظِلُّهُمُ اللَّهُ عَزَّ وَجَلَّ
يَوْمَ الْقِيَامَةِ يَوْمَ لاَ ظِلَّ إِلاَّ ظِلُّهُ إِمَامٌ عَادِلٌ وَشَابٌّ نَشَأَ فِي عِبَادَةِ
اللَّهِ عَزَّ وَجَلَّ وَرَجُلٌ ذَكَرَ اللَّهَ فِي خَلاَءٍ فَفَاضَتْ عَيْنَاهُ وَرَجُلٌ كَانَ
قَلْبُهُ مُعَلَّقًا فِي الْمَسْجِدِ وَرَجُلاَنِ تَحَابَّا فِي اللَّهِ عَزَّ وَجَلَّ وَرَجُلٌ
دَعَتْهُ امْرَأَةٌ ذَاتُ مَنْصِبٍ وَجَمَالٍ إِلَى نَفْسِهَا فَقَالَ إِنِّي أَخَافُ اللَّهَ
عَزَّ وَجَلَّ وَرَجُلٌ تَصَدَّقَ بِصَدَقَةٍ فَأَخْفَاهَا حَتَّى لاَ تَعْلَمَ شِمَالُهُ مَا
صَنَعَتْ يَمِينُهُ

Abū Hurayrah ﷺ narrated that the Messenger of Allah ﷺ said: 'There are seven whom Allah, the Mighty and Sublime, will shade with His shade on the Day of Resurrection, the Day when there will be no shade but His: A just ruler; a young man who grows up worshipping

Allah; a man who remembers Allah when he is alone and his eyes flow (with tears); a man whose heart is attached to the mosque; two men who love each other for the sake of Allah; a man who is called (to commit sin) by a woman of high status and beauty, but he says: "I fear Allah"; and a man who gives charity and conceals it, so much that even his left hand does not know what his right hand is doing.'

The Day of Judgement has been described in the Qur'an and Sunnah with intricate detail. A clear picture has been painted about this great day and how people will feel. It is described as a day of distress, regret, fear, confusion, and discomfort in scorching heat. A day in which humankind will be so worried that they will not be concerned about being naked and unclothed. On that day, humankind will be desperate for something which reduces worry and brings some comfort.

The sun will be only a short distance above people's heads and there will be no shade except for one shade, that of Allah's Throne. On that Day, Allah will shade some people under His throne, so that they are not harmed by the closeness of the sun and the sweltering heat. Allah wills that these people deserve to be bestowed with comfort on such a difficult day because they did some noble actions purely for the sake of Allah. Allah says in the Qur'an: *'Those who believed and did not tarnish their faith with wrongdoing; for them there is security, and it is they who have been guided to the right way'* (*al-An'ām* 6: 82).

One common theme found in each of the categories mentioned in the hadith is that they are people who were willing to give up worldly pleasure and comfort for the sake of the afterlife. Thus, in return, they will be given added comfort in the next life.

The just ruler could easily be led to mistreating others thinking that this would further establish his authority. However, he does not do so because he fears Allah. Just leadership usually only stems from a pure heart.

The young man who grows up worshipping Allah, the man whose heart is attached to the mosque, and he who refuses to fall prey to the trap of a beautiful woman's lure, all gave up the many pleasures that most young people are indulged in, for the sake of Allah. These things require a commendable amount of discipline and consciousness of Allah, especially for those who are young.

Similarly, those who love one another only for the sake of Allah have given preference to the afterlife over this one, while most people only seem to be interested in friendships that can bring them some material gain, such as wealth, status, or a job. The same is said about the sincere worshipper who sheds tears privately; not to show off to others, but out of the genuine feeling of Allah's greatness. Discipline, *taqwa*, and prioritising the afterlife are the traits of these categories of people for which reason they have earned comfort on the Day of Judgement.

How to Solve Problems

عَنْ شُرَيْحٍ أَنَّهُ كَتَبَ إِلَى عُمَرَ يَسْأَلُهُ فَكَتَبَ إِلَيْهِ أَنِ اقْضِ بِمَا فِي كِتَابِ اللَّهِ فَإِنْ لَمْ يَكُنْ فِي كِتَابِ اللَّهِ فَبِسُنَّةِ رَسُولِ اللَّهِ ﷺ فَإِنْ لَمْ يَكُنْ فِي كِتَابِ اللَّهِ وَلاَ فِي سُنَّةِ رَسُولِ اللَّهِ ﷺ فَاقْضِ بِمَا قَضَى بِهِ الصَّالِحُونَ فَإِنْ لَمْ يَكُنْ فِي كِتَابِ اللَّهِ وَلاَ فِي سُنَّةِ رَسُولِ اللَّهِ ﷺ وَلَمْ يَقْضِ بِهِ الصَّالِحُونَ فَإِنْ شِئْتَ فَتَقَدَّمْ وَإِنْ شِئْتَ فَتَأَخَّرْ وَلاَ أَرَى التَّأَخُّرَ إِلاَّ خَيْرًا لَكَ وَالسَّلاَمُ عَلَيْكُمْ

Shurayḥ narrated that he wrote to Umar رضي الله عنه to ask him a question, and Umar رضي الله عنه wrote back telling him: 'Judge according to what is in the Book of Allah. If it is not in the Book of Allah, then (judge) according to the Sunnah of the Messenger of Allah ﷺ. If it is not in the Book of Allah or the Sunnah of the Messenger of Allah ﷺ, then pass judgment according to the way the righteous passed judgment. If it is not in the Book of Allah, or the Sunnah of the Messenger of Allah ﷺ, and the righteous did not pass judgment concerning it, then if you wish, go ahead (and try to work it out by yourself) or if you wish, leave it. And I see that leaving it is better for you. And peace be upon you.'

This statement by the rightly guided Caliph Umar ibn al-Khaṭṭāb ؓ provides the legal basis for every jurist, mufti, and *qāḍī* (judge). Any person attributing something to Islam must have a basis for that, including scholars. Merely being a scholar of Islam does not give one the right to speak without evidence from the Qur'an or the Sunnah. It is only the words of Allah and His Prophet ﷺ that are binding upon every Muslim to follow. The views of anyone besides them, no matter how knowledgeable they are can be wrong and therefore do not have to be followed by every Muslim. Hence, not everything which is attributed to Islam is necessarily a correct attribution, particularly when so many people who have little knowledge of Islam attribute things to Islam. However, if a trusted and qualified scholar gives a ruling (fatwa) then it is permissible for the layperson to follow them.

The Qur'an, being the Word of Allah, is the first and most important source of knowledge. It contains all the guidance needed by humankind. The teachings of the Qur'an can be explicit or implicit, concise or detailed. Therefore, that which is explicit and clear in the Qur'an should be followed without needing any other proof. If, however, something is not mentioned explicitly or in detail, then we should refer to the Prophet's teachings since they are an explanation of the Qur'an. That which is mentioned in the Qur'an in a general sense or is open to interpretation is clarified by the Prophet ﷺ, either verbally or practically. If something is not mentioned clearly in the Qur'an or the Sunnah, then we will most likely find it implicitly mentioned in the Qur'an and Sunnah, if enough time is spent studying it and pondering over it.

Finally, if we can't accurately understand or interpret the implicit texts mentioned in the Qur'an and the Sunnah, then as Umar ﷺ encouraged Shurayḥ to do when something was not clear to him, we must refer to the understanding of the Companions and the righteous people. That is because their knowledge of the language and context of the Qur'an was greatest; they accompanied the Prophet ﷺ and they were greater in piety, which makes them more likely to have sound understanding of Islam. These guidelines are the right way to understand what Islam teaches us. Not following these steps will most certainly lead to error in understanding Islam and solving Islamic problems.

The concluding statement of 'Umar's advice is referring to *ijtihad* or juristic reasoning. This is when a qualified scholar exercises reasoning to deduce Islamic edicts from the sources of Muslim law. Only a qualified person may engage in *ijtihad* and that is probably why 'Umar told Shurayḥ that it was better for him not to engage in *ijtihad* because he was uncertain if Shurayḥ was qualified or competent to do so. The reason why it is a serious matter is because giving a wrong opinion about Islamic matters when a person is not fully qualified to do so is sinful and can mislead people. This is why it is important for Muslims to follow the opinions of qualified and righteous scholars.

32

What to Recite for Protection and Help

عَنْ مُعَاذِ بْنِ عَبْدِ اللَّهِ بن خبيب عَنْ أَبِيهِ قَالَ أَصَابَنَا طَشٌّ
وَظُلْمَةٌ فَانْتَظَرْنَا رَسُولَ اللَّهِ ﷺ لِيُصَلِّيَ بِنَا ثُمَّ ذَكَرَ كَلَامًا مَعْنَاهُ
فَخَرَجَ رَسُولُ اللَّهِ ﷺ لِيُصَلِّيَ بِنَا فَقَالَ قُلْ فَقُلْتُ مَا أَقُولُ
قَالَ قُلْ هُوَ اللَّهُ أَحَدٌ وَالْمُعَوِّذَتَيْنِ حِينَ تُمْسِي وَحِينَ تُصْبِحُ
ثَلَاثًا يَكْفِيكَ كُلَّ شَيْءٍ

It was narrated from Muʿādh ibn ʿAbdullāh ibn Khubayb that his father said: 'It was raining and dark, and we were waiting for the Messenger of Allah ﷺ to lead us in prayer. Then the Messenger of Allah ﷺ came out to lead us in prayer and he said: "Say." I said: What should I say? He said: "Say: He is Allah, (the) One and *al-Muʿawwidhatayn* in the evening and in the morning, three times, and that will suffice you against everything."'

What truly protects a person in this life is their strong faith (*īmān*) in Allah. Their knowledge and belief that benefit and harm can only occur with the permission of Allah. However, the Prophet Muhammad ﷺ taught us to recite certain verses of the Qur'an due to a specific virtue that they have. This is not because they act as a magic cure for things—because the Qur'an was never revealed for this purpose—rather, because of the meanings contained in these verses.

The last three chapters of the Qur'an have a particular importance because they summarise the concept of sincerity and total reliance (*tawakkul*) upon Allah. When reciting these verses with understanding, we are reminding ourselves that only Allah is worthy of being truly feared and that He alone is able to do what He wills. In the first of these three chapters, *Surah al-Ikhlāṣ* (Chapter of Sincerity), Allah says: *'Allah, who is in need of none and of whom all are in need... and none is comparable to him.'* In *Surah al-Falaq*, Allah says: *'Say, I seek refuge with the Lord of the falaq (rising day); from the evil of all that He created.'* In *Surah al-Nās*, He says: *'Say, I seek refuge in the Lord of humankind...from the evil of the retreating whisperer.'* Because of the nature of the verses in the last two chapters of the Qur'an, they are known as *al-Mu'awwidhatayn*, i.e., verses of refuge.

These verses remind us that our needs should be sought only from the One who is free of needs, not from others who are as equally needy as ourselves. They remind us that whatever harm or evil that exists, it is Allah whom we seek refuge and protection from evil in. These meanings of firm belief and a true understanding of who Allah is make these chapters so important. Simply reciting chosen verses will not have the same impact. However, when we recite these chapters on a regular basis, with understanding and certainty in the promise of Allah, we instil in ourselves a total reliance upon Allah which protects us from harm and keeps our hearts content at times of tribulation. It is of great benefit to practise this hadith and to read the last three chapters of the Qur'an regularly.

33

Seeking Refuge in Allah from Hardship and Doing Wrong

عَنْ أَبِي هُرَيْرَةَ أَنَّ النَّبِيَّ صلى الله عليه وسلم كَانَ يَقُولُ اللَّهُمَّ إِنِّي أَعُوذُ بِكَ مِنَ الْقِلَّةِ وَالْفَقْرِ وَالذِّلَّةِ وَأَعُوذُ بِكَ أَنْ أَظْلِمَ أَوْ أُظْلَمَ

Abū Hurayrah ﵁ narrated that the Prophet ﷺ used to say: '*Allāhumma innī a'ūdhu bika minal-qillati wal-faqr, wadh-dhillati wa a'ūdhu bika an aẓlima aw uẓlam*' (O Allah, I seek refuge with You from want, poverty, and humiliation, and I seek refuge with You from wronging others or being wronged).'

Imam al-Nasā'ī in his book, *Al-Sunan*, mentioned a whole chapter on the things the Prophet ﷺ used to seek refuge from in his supplications. In this hadith, Abū Hurayrah ﵁ tells us that the Prophet Muhammad ﷺ used to seek refuge in Allah from having 'little' (*qillah*) and poverty (*faqr*).

One interpretation of 'poverty' is having little wealth. That is because when one is in financial difficulty, they may constantly find themselves occupied with thinking about money, lacking contentment, and possibly even having to ask others, which can lead to humiliation and being belittled. However, this is not a general rule. There are those who are poor, but are satisfied and rich at heart. They never feel the need to look at what others have and are content with what Allah has given them. Therefore, poverty in the Prophet's *du'ā'* here could have another meaning; that is to not be content. This is a poverty of the heart. The Prophet ﷺ said: '[True] richness is the richness of the self.'[10] This means that one is content with Allah and is free of needing others. It is a disaster to have plenty of money, and never be satisfied. When the heart is in such a state of poverty, it also leads to humiliation in this life because they were not content with what Allah gave them and were always after more.

In this supplication, the Prophet Muhammad ﷺ also sought refuge from oppressing others or being oppressed. That is because oppression is a darkness and an injustice. The oppressor will not be able to escape retribution until the oppressed takes their full right from the oppressor or forgives them, either in this life or the next. Injustice and oppression are therefore from the worst of sins, and every Muslim is required to avoid it to the best of their ability.

This supplication can be said at any time. It is always best to use the wording that the Prophet ﷺ used, but this is not obligatory. One can supplicate to Allah using the same meanings contained in this *du'ā'*, even in their own language.

---

10 Muslim, *Sahih Muslim*, Hadith no. 1051

34

The Three Du'ā's *of Prophet Sulayman*

عَنْ عَبْدِ اللَّهِ بْنِ عَمْرٍو عَنْ رَسُولِ اللَّهِ ﷺ أَنَّ سُلَيْمَانَ بْنَ دَاوُدَ ﷺ لَمَّا بَنَى بَيْتَ الْمَقْدِسِ سَأَلَ اللَّهَ عَزَّ وَجَلَّ خِلاَلاً ثَلاَثَةً سَأَلَ اللَّهَ عَزَّ وَجَلَّ حُكْمًا يُصَادِفُ حُكْمَهُ فَأُوتِيَهُ وَسَأَلَ اللَّهَ عَزَّ وَجَلَّ مُلْكًا لاَ يَنْبَغِي لأَحَدٍ مِنْ بَعْدِهِ فَأُوتِيَهُ وَسَأَلَ اللَّهَ عَزَّ وَجَلَّ حِينَ فَرَغَ مِنْ بِنَاءِ الْمَسْجِدِ أَنْ لاَ يَأْتِيَهُ أَحَدٌ لاَ يَنْهَزُهُ إِلاَّ الصَّلاَةُ فِيهِ أَنْ يُخْرِجَهُ مِنْ خَطِيئَتِهِ كَيَوْمِ وَلَدَتْهُ أُمُّهُ

'Abdullāh ibn 'Amr رضي الله عنه reported that the Messenger of Allah ﷺ said: 'When Sulaymān ibn Dāwūd finished building Bayt al-Maqdis, he asked Allah for three things: Judgement that was in harmony with Allah's judgement, and he was given that. He asked Allah for a dominion that no one after him would have, and he was given that.

When he finished building the Masjid al-Aqṣā, he asked
Allah, the Mighty and Sublime, that no one should come
to it, intending only to pray there, except that he would
emerge free of sin as the day his mother bore him.'

The Prophet Sulaymān ※ was one of the great Prophets of Allah.
In the Bible, he is known as Solomon, the son of David. He
was blessed by Allah with many virtues, one of which was the ability
to talk to animals and insects, control the wind and talk to the jinn.
Allah mentions in the Qurʾan about some of the forms of power and
authority that were given to Prophet Sulaymān ※: *'We subjected to
him the wind, blowing gently at his command to wherever he pleased.
And [We subjected to him] every builder and diver of the* jinn*'* (*Ṣād* 38:
36–37).

Prophets are special people to Allah; so when they make *duʿāʾ*
to Allah, He pays special attention to their requests. When Prophet
Sulaymān ※ asked Allah to grant him three things, Allah accepted his
duʿāʾ and granted them to him. The Qurʾan informs us that he was
given an exceptional understanding and ability to judge correctly.
When speaking of Dāwūd and Sulaymān ※, Allah says: *'We guided
Sulaymān to the right verdict, and we granted each of them judgment
and knowledge'* (*al-Anbiyāʾ* 21: 79). Sulaymān ※ also supplicated to
Allah for a powerful kingdom and a supreme reign. The Qurʾan relates:
*'My Lord, forgive me and bestow upon me a kingdom such as none other
after me will have'* (*Ṣād* 38: 35).

An interesting incident took place during the time of the Prophet
Muhammad ※ while he was in prayer. It is reported in Ṣaḥīḥ al-
Bukhārī and Ṣaḥīḥ Muslim that the Prophet ※ said: 'A devil from the
jinn came to me to spoil my prayer, but Allah enabled me to overpower
him, and so I caught him and intended to tie him to one of the pillars
of the mosque so that all of you might see him, but I remembered the

invocation of my brother Sulaymān: *'And grant me a kingdom such as shall not belong to any other after me,'* so I let him go.'

The first two requests Sulaymān ﷺ made were particular to him, but the third was extended to include everyone visiting Masjid al-Aqṣā. Allah commanded the Prophet Sulaymān ﷺ to build Masjid al-Aqṣā. This mosque has a special place in Islam whereby it was the first direction of prayer and the third holiest mosque, for the Muslims. Moreover, the Prophet Sulaymān ﷺ asked Allah to grant the person visiting the mosque, solely intending to pray there, to be free of sin as the day their mother gave birth to them.

This is amazing news for those people who can visit Masjid al-Aqṣā. However, since not everyone will be able to visit Masjid al-Aqṣā, Allah has bestowed a similar blessing for Muslims at every mosque. That is to say, the Prophet ﷺ told us that the one who performs ablution well, then makes his way to the mosque only intending to pray and not being distracted by anything else, would be forgiven and have their rank raised with every step they take to the mosque. If one can pray at Masjid al-Aqṣā then this is certainly greater, and the reward of praying there is multiplied significantly.

35

Forgetting to Pray

عَنْ أَبِي هُرَيْرَةَ أَنَّ رَسُولَ اللَّهِ ﷺ قَالَ مَنْ نَسِيَ صَلاَةً فَلْيُصَلِّهَا إِذَا ذَكَرَهَا فَإِنَّ اللَّهَ تَعَالَى قَالَ أَقِمِ الصَّلاَةَ لِذِكْرِي

Abū Hurayrah ﵁ said that the Messenger of Allah ﷺ said: 'Whoever forgets a prayer, let him pray it when he remembers it, for Allah says: "*...and perform the ṣalāh for My remembrance*" (*Ṭā Hā* 20: 14).'

Prayer is one of the greatest acts of worship that the Qur'an has emphasised. So long as a Muslim is consistently performing their five daily prayers on time, they have a strong rope which connects them to Allah; one which will ultimately provide them with safety and victory in this life and the next. It is not sufficient to simply perform prayers, but they must be performed at their specified time; neither before nor after. The Qur'an states: *'Indeed, performing prayers is a duty on the believers at the appointed times'* (*al-Nisā'* 4: 103). These times were alluded to in the Qur'an, but further clarified in the Prophetic Sunnah. There are some situations in which it is permissible to combine the noon prayer (Ẓuhr) with the afternoon prayer ('Aṣr) or the evening prayer at sunset (Maghrib) with the night prayer ('Ishā'). Besides this, it is not permissible to delay a prayer beyond its specified time. However, as with all obligations in Islam, Allah has forgiven and overlooked actions which occur due to forgetfulness or due to reasons beyond one's control.

Allah has demanded that prayer be offered at all times and during all circumstances. If someone completely forgets to pray or was asleep until the time of prayer had ended, they would not be sinful. This is because it was not their intention to delay the prayer beyond its appointed time. In this case, the Prophet Muhammad ﷺ directed us to perform the prayer as soon as we remember, regardless of whatever time it is.

Precaution should always be taken to ensure that one is able to perform prayer on time. This is especially required in the case of the Fajr prayer, as it is the prayer that is most likely to be missed. We must make sure to sleep on time to ensure that we are able to wake up for the Fajr prayer. However, forgetfulness and sleep can occur despite that, as they did to the Prophet ﷺ himself, despite appointing Bilāl ﷺ to wake everyone up. However, Bilāl ﷺ overslept too, so the Prophet ﷺ simply prayed in congregation the way he normally prayed as soon as he woke up.[11] It is wrong to make no attempt to wake up for Fajr prayer or succumb to laziness. It is only when a person misses Fajr prayer accidently that they will not be held accountable.

11 Al-Bukhari, *Sahih al-Bukhari*, Hadith no. 569

Greeting Friends in Prayer

عَنْ جَابِرِ بْنِ سَمُرَةَ قَالَ كُنَّا نُصَلِّي خَلْفَ النَّبِيِّ ﷺ فَنُسَلِّمُ بِأَيْدِينَا فَقَالَ مَا بَالُ هَؤُلَاءِ يُسَلِّمُونَ بِأَيْدِيهِمْ كَأَنَّهَا أَذْنَابُ خَيْلٍ شُمْسٍ أَمَا يَكْفِي أَحَدَهُمْ أَنْ يَضَعَ يَدَهُ عَلَى فَخِذِهِ ثُمَّ يَقُولَ السَّلَامُ عَلَيْكُمْ السَّلَامُ عَلَيْكُمْ

It was narrated that Jābir ibn Samurah ﵁ said: 'We used to pray behind the Messenger of Allah ﷺ and we would greet each other with our hands. He said: "What is the matter with those who greet with their hands as if they were tails of wild horses? It is sufficient for one to put his hand on his thigh and say: *As-salāmu 'alaykum, as-salāmu 'alaykum.*"'

Jābir ibn Samurah ؓ explains that some of the Muslims at the time of the Prophet ﷺ, upon ending the prayer and reciting the *salām*, would greet those to their left and right by raising and waving their hands. The Prophet Muhammad ﷺ then explained to them that it was sufficient for them to say the *salām* while keeping their hands on their thighs. Waving their hands was likened to the fast movement of the tails of wild horses, which contradicts the tranquillity and calmness that should be upheld during the prayer.

Zayd ibn Arqam ؓ reports that when the prayer was first legislated, the Companions would speak to one another during the prayer. This was the case until Allah revealed, *'Take due care of the prayers, and the middle prayer [in particular], and stand before Allah in total devotion'* (*al-Baqarah* 2: 238). Zayd explained that when this verse was revealed, they were commanded to remain silent in the prayer. That is because total silence and focus is what befits standing in front of Allah.

This hadith not only teaches us that unnecessary movement during the prayer should be avoided, but also that all movements of the prayer should be done with tranquillity and calmness. There are times during the prayer when the Prophet ﷺ would raise both his hands up to around his shoulders, such as at the start of the prayer, before *rukūʿ* (bowing), and after *rukūʿ*. Even this should be done in a calm and controlled way. Similarly, when going into prostration, one should not drop themselves to the ground, but rather make their way down slowly. The Companions also described the recitation of the Prophet ﷺ as being a controlled one. He would recite verse by verse, stopping at the end of each verse. These are merely examples which show that the whole prayer of the Prophet ﷺ was done in this manner. Anything which contradicts calmness, tranquillity, and focus should be avoided.

ﷻ

37

Islam: The Complete Religion

عَنْ طَارِقِ بْنِ شِهَابٍ قَالَ جَاءَ رَجُلٌ مِنَ الْيَهُودِ إِلَى عُمَرَ بْنِ
الْخَطَّابِ فَقَالَ يَا أَمِيرَ الْمُؤْمِنِينَ آيَةٌ فِى كِتَابِكُمْ تَقْرَءُونَهَا لَوْ
عَلَيْنَا مَعْشَرَ الْيَهُودِ نَزَلَتْ لَاتَّخَذْنَا ذَلِكَ الْيَوْمَ عِيدًا قَالَ أَىُّ آيَةٍ
قَالَ الْيَوْمَ أَكْمَلْتُ لَكُمْ دِينَكُمْ وَأَتْمَمْتُ عَلَيْكُمْ نِعْمَتِى
وَرَضِيتُ لَكُمُ الْإِسْلَامَ دِينًا فَقَالَ عُمَرُ إِنِّى لَأَعْلَمُ الْمَكَانَ الَّذِى
نَزَلَتْ فِيهِ وَالْيَوْمَ الَّذِى نَزَلَتْ فِيهِ نَزَلَتْ عَلَى رَسُولِ اللَّهِ ﷺ فِى
عَرَفَاتٍ فِى يَوْمِ جُمُعَةٍ

It was narrated that Ṭāriq ibn Shihāb said: 'A Jewish man came to Umar ibn al-Khaṭṭāb and said: "O Commander of the Believers! There is a verse in your Book which you recite; if it had been revealed to us Jews, we would have taken that day as a festival." He said: "Which verse is that?" He said: *"This day, I have perfected your religion for you, completed My favour upon you, and have chosen for you Islam as your religion."*[12] Umar said: "I know the place where it was revealed and the day on which it was revealed. It was revealed to the Messenger of Allah ﷺ at 'Arafāt, on a Friday."'

"This day, I have perfected your religion for you, completed My favour upon you, and have chosen for you Islam as your religion."

This great verse of Surah al-Mā'idah is one which should remind every Muslim of the blessing of Islam. How incredible is it to know that one is following the way that Allah wants them to follow in their life! A way that has been completed and requires no addition. This verse provides an unambiguous message stating that what Allah has revealed is all that we need to be guided in this life and the next. Imam Mālik ibn Anas is reported to have used this verse to reject innovated practices in Islam. Anyone who adds to what the Prophet ﷺ brought is implying that the religion is incomplete. Thus, that which was not part of the Islam then cannot be part of Islam now. There is no blessing greater than guidance. The persistent challenges of life can certainly be burdensome and overwhelming. But as long as one has a heart filled with conviction and faith in their principles, it becomes easier to face whatever life throws in their direction.

Some of the Jews at the time of Umar ﵁ understood the

---

12 Qur'an 5:3

significance of such a verse. They considered the revelation of such a magnificent verse worthy of celebration. When a Jewish man expressed these feelings, Umar ﷠ explained that he too knows the significance of this verse, which was why he remembered the exact day and place of its revelation. That was on the day of 'Arafah, Friday the 9th of Dhū al-Ḥijjah in the 10th year after the Hijrah of the Prophet ﷺ to Madinah. This was when the Prophet ﷺ performed his only hajj pilgrimage in the presence of thousands of Muslims. It was the final opportunity for him to address such a large congregation of Muslims, leaving behind some golden reminders, and leaving behind this verse which Muslims can be grateful for until the end of time.

Abu Bakr and the Prophet ﷺ as Imam

عَنْ سَهْلِ بْنِ سَعْدٍ قَالَ انْطَلَقَ رَسُولُ اللَّهِ ﷺ يُصْلِحُ بَيْنَ بَنِي عَمْرِو بْنِ عَوْفٍ فَحَضَرَتِ الصَّلاَةُ فَجَاءَ الْمُؤَذِّنُ إِلَى أَبِي بَكْرٍ فَأَمَرَهُ أَنْ يَجْمَعَ النَّاسَ وَيَؤُمَّهُمْ فَجَاءَ رَسُولُ اللَّهِ ﷺ فَخَرَقَ الصُّفُوفَ حَتَّى قَامَ فِي الصَّفِّ الْمُقَدَّمِ ۝ وَصَفَّحَ النَّاسُ بِأَبِي بَكْرٍ لِيُؤْذِنُوهُ بِرَسُولِ اللَّهِ ﷺ وَكَانَ أَبُو بَكْرٍ لاَ يَلْتَفِتُ فِي الصَّلاَةِ ۝ فَلَمَّا أَكْثَرُوا عَلِمَ أَنَّهُ قَدْ نَابَهُمْ شَيْءٌ فِي صَلاَتِهِمْ فَالْتَفَتَ فَإِذَا هُوَ بِرَسُولِ اللَّهِ ﷺ فَأَوْمَأَ إِلَيْهِ رَسُولُ اللَّهِ ﷺ أَيْ كَمَا أَنْتَ فَرَفَعَ أَبُو بَكْرٍ يَدَيْهِ فَحَمِدَ اللَّهَ وَأَثْنَى عَلَيْهِ لِقَوْلِ رَسُولِ اللَّهِ ﷺ ثُمَّ رَجَعَ الْقَهْقَرَى وَتَقَدَّمَ رَسُولُ اللَّهِ ﷺ فَصَلَّى فَلَمَّا انْصَرَفَ قَالَ لأَبِي بَكْرٍ مَا مَنَعَكَ إِذْ أَوْمَأْتُ إِلَيْكَ أَنْ تُصَلِّيَ ۝ فَقَالَ أَبُو بَكْرٍ رضي الله عنه مَا كَانَ يَنْبَغِي لاِبْنِ أَبِي قُحَافَةَ أَنْ يَؤُمَّ رَسُولَ اللَّهِ ﷺ ثُمَّ قَالَ

لِلنَّاسِ مَا بَالُكُمْ صَفَّحْتُمْ إِنَّمَا التَّصْفِيحُ لِلنِّسَاءِ ثُمَّ قَالَ إِذَا نَابَكُمْ شَيْءٌ فِي صَلاَتِكُمْ فَسَبِّحُوا

It was narrated that Sahl ibn Saʿd ؓ said: 'The Messenger of Allah ﷺ set out to bring about reconciliation among Banū ʿAmr ibn ʿAwf. The time for prayer came, and the muezzin (caller to the prayer) went to Abu Bakr to tell him to gather the people and lead them in prayer. Then the Messenger of Allah ﷺ came and passed though the rows until he stood in the first row. The people started clapping to let Abu Bakr know that the Messenger of Allah ﷺ had come. Abu Bakr never used to turn around when he prayed, but when they clapped consistently, he realised something must have happened while they were praying. So, he turned around and saw the Messenger of Allah ﷺ. The Messenger of Allah ﷺ gestured to him to stay where he was. Abu Bakr raised his hands and praised and thanked Allah for what the Messenger of Allah ﷺ had said. Then he moved backwards, and the Messenger of Allah ﷺ went forward and prayed. When he finished, he said to Abu Bakr: "What stopped you from continuing to pray when I gestured to you?" Abu Bakr ؓ said: "It was not appropriate for the son of Abū Quḥāfah to lead the Messenger of Allah in prayer." Then he said to the people:

"Why did you clap? Clapping is for women." Then he said: "If you notice something when you are praying, say '*Subḥānallāh.*'"

The Prophet ﷺ taught the Companions the importance of praying on time. Therefore, when they felt that he may not attend due to being occupied with mediation and helping people settle their differences, they requested Abu Bakr ؓ to go forth and lead the Muslims in prayer. They made this decision because the Prophet ﷺ ordered that Abu Bakr ؓ should lead the prayer during his illness. The Companions knew the status of Abu Bakr ؓ with the Prophet ﷺ and would therefore always view him as the Prophet's deputy. His close companionship with the Prophet Muhammad ﷺ meant that he was most knowledgeable of the Sunnah and most worthy of taking on the role of imam in the absence of the Prophet ﷺ. This is why the Muslims did not have any doubt about Abu Bakr ؓ being the Caliph of the Muslims after the Prophet ﷺ, and the Prophet ﷺ himself knew that the Muslims would not choose anyone other than him, as reported in Ṣaḥīḥ al-Bukhārī.

When Abu Bakr ؓ became aware of the Prophet's attendance while he was leading the prayer, he did not feel it acceptable to stand in front of the Prophet ﷺ in prayer, so he decided to step back and make way for the Prophet Muhammad ﷺ. Although the Prophet ﷺ wanted him to continue leading the prayer, this change of imam did not impact the validity of the prayer, because the Prophet ﷺ was the main imam, along with the special status that he had. When Abu Bakr saw that the Prophet ﷺ told him to remain in his place, he raised his hands praising Allah for the correct decision that he and the Muslims had made. After the prayer, the Prophet ﷺ told the Companions that when something needs be pointed out during the prayer or an error is made by the imam, the men should say '*subḥānallāh*' in order to make the imam aware. They should avoid clapping because this leads to movement and possible confusion. However, if women want to point something out during prayer, they should clap slightly while making as little movement as possible. This is so that they do not have to resort to raising their voices, particularly if they are a distance away from the imam in the rows behind.

The Best Fast and the Best Prayer

عَنْ أَبِي هُرَيْرَةَ قَالَ قَالَ رَسُولُ اللَّهِ ﷺ أَفْضَلُ الصِّيَامِ بَعْدَ شَهْرِ رَمَضَانَ شَهْرُ اللَّهِ الْمُحَرَّمُ وَأَفْضَلُ الصَّلَاةِ بَعْدَ الْفَرِيضَةِ صَلَاةُ اللَّيْلِ

Abū Hurayrah ﵁ reported that the Messenger of Allah ﷺ said: 'The best fasting after the month of Ramadan is the month of Allah, Muharram, and the best prayer is prayer at night.'

Everything Allah has made compulsory such as prayer and fasting is most beloved to Allah. Besides the obligation of praying five times a day and fasting the month of Ramadan, the Prophet ﷺ would regularly pray during the day and night and fast throughout the year. It is reported that Anas ibn Mālik said, 'The Messenger of Allah ﷺ used to leave off fasting during a month until we thought that he would not fast at all during it; and (sometimes) he would fast till we began to think that he would not omit any day of that month.

If one wished to see him performing prayer during the night, he could do that; and if one wished to see him sleeping at night, he could do that.' This statement from Anas shows how consistent and balanced the Prophet ﷺ was with his worship. The Prophet ﷺ was generally consistent with his worship without normally specifying particular times or days at which he had to pray or fast. However, there were certain times during which he particularly encouraged people to pray and fast.

In this hadith, fasting the month of Muharram (the first month of the Islamic calendar) and praying during the night were considered the best times to fast and pray. The day of Ashura, the 10th of Muharram, was consistently fasted by the Prophet ﷺ, and he encouraged the Muslims to do so. It is also recommended to fast additional days throughout this month. Regarding the night prayer, the Prophet ﷺ was so consistent with it that he would sometimes be told by his wives and the Companions to take things easy on himself; and the Prophet ﷺ would reply to them saying, 'Should I not be a thankful servant?'

Some scholars considered the night prayer (*qiyām al-layl*) to be obligatory upon the Prophet ﷺ since the Qur'an specifically commanded him to do so in *Surah al-Muzzammil*. Although the scholars agree that it is not an obligation upon the Muslims in general, they agree that the night prayer is one of the greatest acts of worship. Besides the fact that it is a Sunnah of the Prophet Muhammad ﷺ and the Prophets before him, the night prayer is one of the best ways to develop sincerity and attain closeness to Allah. It can be performed at any time after 'Ishā' prayer, and the Prophet ﷺ sometimes performed it at the start, sometimes in the middle, and sometimes towards the end of the night. However, eventually he would consistently perform it towards the end of the night, as that is the most blessed time to pray and to remember Allah. One can begin by praying two or four units before they sleep, until they gradually practise praying towards the latter part of the night, which is the best time for the night prayer.

40

Treating All Your Children Equally

عن النُّعْمَانُ بْنُ بَشِيرٍ أَنَّ أُمَّهُ ابْنَةَ رَوَاحَةَ سَأَلَتْ أَبَاهُ بَعْضَ الْمَوْهِبَةِ مِنْ مَالِهِ لاِبْنِهَا فَالْتَوَى بِهَا سَنَةً ثُمَّ بَدَا لَهُ فَوَهَبَهَا لَهُ فَقَالَتْ لاَ أَرْضَى حَتَّى تُشْهِدَ رَسُولَ اللَّهِ ﷺ فَقَالَ يَا رَسُولَ اللَّهِ إِنَّ أُمَّ هَذَا ابْنَةَ رَوَاحَةَ قَاتَلَتْنِي عَلَى الَّذِى وَهَبْتُ لَهُ فَقَالَ رَسُولُ اللَّهِ ﷺ يَا بَشِيرُ أَلَكَ وَلَدٌ سِوَى هَذَا؟ قَالَ نَعَمْ فَقَالَ رَسُولُ اللَّهِ ﷺ أَفَكُلَّهُمْ وَهَبْتَ لَهُمْ مِثْلَ الَّذِى وَهَبْتَ لاِبْنِكَ هَذَا قَالَ لاَ قَالَ رَسُولُ اللَّهِ ﷺ فَلاَ تُشْهِدْنِي إِذًا فَإِنِّي لاَ أَشْهَدُ عَلَى جَوْرٍ

Nu'mān ibn Bashīr ؓ narrated that his mother, the daughter of Rawāḥah, asked his father to give some of his wealth to her son. He deferred that for a year, then he decided to give it to him. She said: 'I will not be pleased until you ask the Messenger of Allah ﷺ to bear witness.'

He said: 'O Messenger of Allah, the mother of this boy, the daughter of Rawāḥah, insisted that I consult you first about giving a gift to him.' The Messenger of Allah ﷺ said: 'O Bashīr, do you have any other children besides this one?' He said: 'Yes.' The Messenger of Allah ﷺ said: 'Have you given all of them a gift like that which you have given to this son of yours?' He said: 'No.' The Messenger of Allah ﷺ said: 'Then do not ask me to bear witness, for I will not bear witness to unfairness.'

This hadith is a profoundly important lesson to all parents. Children are a grave responsibility upon parents. The Prophet ﷺ told us that each of us will be questioned about those we are responsible for. This not only includes providing them with the best upbringing and education, but also treating them well. Just as children must treat their parents with excellence and kindness, parents also have a responsibility to be kind and fair with their children. The general rule when it comes to giving gifts and spending on one's children is that they should be treated equally. This general rule was laid down by the Prophet ﷺ in the incident mentioned above. In fact, the Prophet ﷺ considered unequally distributing gifts to children to be a form of injustice for which he refused to be a witness. It is quite clear that giving gifts to some of your children while leaving others out or giving them less can become a cause of ill feelings, envy, and dispute between siblings and parents.

The scenario in which the Prophet ﷺ made this statement appears to be one in which one child was chosen to be given a gift for no valid reason, and hence the injustice. However, if children are of different ages, at different stages of life, or have special needs, then there is no harm in giving children according to their individual needs and circumstances. It could be that a parent gifts the children according to what suits their age and phase in life. This is something that most parents appreciate. It would not be blameworthy to do so because overall, the parent is treating the children in the same manner, but only choosing the appropriate time to give the most suitable gifts. If one gave their twenty-year-old child a car, they would not need to do so with their five-year-old child. Similarly, a parent may have a child with a disability who requires special attention and additional spending. This falls under the bracket of spending according to need, as opposed to general gifts, hence equal spending is not required. The guiding principle here is that parents should do their best to treat their children the same way and to make them feel that they are loved the same as their siblings.

It is highly objectionable and sinful to give gifts to children simply because of gender, such as preferring boys over girls. In like manner, to choose a 'favourite' child and shower them with gifts with the exclusion of others is not acceptable, rather it is unethical and unlawful.